FAITH
for LIFE

D1506626

Keith A. Butler

word of faith
INT'L CHRISTIAN CENTER

20000 W. Nine Mile Road • Southfield, MI 48075
Pastor André Butler, Senior Pastor
Bishop Keith A. Butler, Founder & Presiding Bishop
Tel.: 248.353.3476 • 24-Hour Prayer: 800.541.PRAY (7729)
To Order: 888.909 WORD (9673)

Faith For Life
Keith A. Butler

ISBN: 978-0-9825692-4-5

Published by
Word of Faith International Christian Center
20000 W. Nine Mile Road
Southfield, Michigan 48075-5597
www.wordoffaith.cc

Printed in the United States of America

CONTENTS

Introduction

The Word tells us that in the last days perilous times will come. I believe that we are in those last days, and the Lord told me that what I am teaching in this book is absolutely critical to your ability to live as an overcomer. Those who know how to walk by faith and not by sight are the ones that will experience victory during these difficult and dangerous times. The Word said, *"This is the victory that overcometh the world, even our faith"* (1 John 5:4).

In *Faith for Life*, I explore the life of Abraham, the most important person in Scripture after the Father, Son and Holy Ghost. Abraham made some mistakes and experienced some failures, but he eventually learned how to live as a man in covenant with God. The works of Abraham and the faith of Abraham are discussed in depth, along with scriptural examples of the ways God speaks to men and women and the things we need to do in order to hear His voice. This skill of hearing the voice of God and then acting upon it will be critical as world systems fail. There will be no middle ground; you will have to be all in for God. The good news is that God is on your side; you are an heir of the blessing, which means that the power of God and the promises of God are yours as you walk by faith.

You will face tests and pressures, but know that through the death and resurrection of Jesus Christ you have been given everything you need to live a life that is pleasing to God. One day, God will honor you as a person who lived by faith. You will receive the reward of Heaven that He has reserved for you.

1

Doing the Works of Abraham

Jesus' message to the people in the temple the last few days before he prayed with tears of agony in the Garden of Gethsemane, died upon the cross, and was raised from the dead was the same message He had been preaching throughout Galilee and Jerusalem. Namely, that the people were the seed of Abraham, and that this entitled them to right-standing with God, the health and healing power of God, and all other things provided by a covenant with God. They were and we are heirs according to the promise.

God the Father, God the Son, and God the Holy Spirit are the most important personages in Scripture. After them, Abraham is a key person, and that is why Jesus mentions him so often.

Jesus often wound up in verbal sparring sessions with the Pharisees in the temple, whereby they attempted to trap him or trick him. Let's look at how Jesus *name of Nahor's wife, Milcah, the daughter of Haran, the father of Milcah, and the father of Iscah. But Sarai was barren; she had no child. And Terah took Abram his son, and Lot the son of Haran his son's son, and Sarai his daughter in law, his son Abram's wife; and they went forth with them from Ur of the Chaldees, to go into the land of Canaan; and they came unto Haran, and dwelt there" (Genesis 11:27-31).*

For some reason, Abraham's father, Terah, decided to leave Ur of Chaldees and go to the land of Canaan. Note that Terah took Abraham, but he did not take Nahor. When they got to Haran, they stopped. Terah died there when he was 205 years old.

Genesis 12:1

Now the LORD had said unto Abram,
Get thee out of thy country, and from
thy kindred, and from thy father's house,
unto a land that I will shew thee.

This verse says that LORD *had* said, past tense. God had spoken to Abraham previously. I am going to use some deductive reasoning, because the Word does not state some things specifically. It appears, however, as if God had spoken to Abraham while in the Ur of Chaldees and that Abraham's father and Lot decided to go with Abraham, even though God had told Abraham to leave this place, his father and his kinfolk. When Terah died, Abraham remembered God's words and started moving again. What do we learn from this?

First, we see that Abraham found it difficult to leave his kinfolk, although the Lord had told him to do so. His father went with him, and Lot went with him. Even after his father died and the Lord clearly said that Abraham was to leave his kindred, Abraham still took Lot. Abraham accepted the call and headed to the Promised Land, but he was delayed and allowed other things to keep him from fully answering the call.

How many people has God called, expecting obedience, who allow family or other circumstances to keep them from doing what God told them to do? Many get delayed, and many never answer the call at all.

It appears as if the Lord came to Abraham a second time. I know that the Lord came to me several times in order to get me to do what was necessary!

Genesis 12:2-5

And I will make of thee a great nation, and I will bless thee, and make thy name great; and thou shalt be a blessing: And I will bless them that bless thee, and curse him that curseth thee: and in thee shall all families of the earth be blessed.

So Abram departed, as the LORD had spoken unto him; and Lot went with him: and Abram was seventy and five years old when he departed out of Haran. And Abram took Sarai his wife, and Lot sessions, packed up and headed toward Palestine. Now think about this. I want you to hear this Scripture as if it were a report from the daily news, not as if it were a fairy tale. In today's news, the headline would be: **Man Walks 400 Miles Across Desert.** The journey was too long to carry all the water and food they'd need. They encountered dangers in the journey such as vipers and poisonous insects.

Many of us, when God speaks, think we have to have a sign or a confirmation that God is talking. We ask for the street to turn to yellow-gold or for five people to prophesy. We want signs every step of the way. Abraham, however, simply set out.

Living With a Single-Minded Focus

Abraham was focused only on one thing. He was imperfect in his execution, but he was single-minded in doing at any cost what God said. Abraham was willing to sacrifice all he had for God. Why was he willing?

Hebrews 11:9-10

By faith he sojourned in the land of promise, as in a strange country, dwelling in tabernacles with Isaac and Jacob, the heirs with him of the same promise: For he looked for a city which hath foundations, whose builder and maker is God.

Abraham was motivated by looking to Heaven. The Bible says this about this hope: *"And every man that hath this hope in him purifieth himself, even as he is pure" (1 John 3:3).*

Even if you were to live 200 years on Earth, next to eternity, that is no time at all. You get caught up in the day-to-day bustle and start thinking that this defines your life. *It doesn't.* You are moving into eternity. You need to keep the following on the forefront of your mind: *"I love my Father, I want to live with Him forever, and He has called me to do a job."* When Heaven is on your mind, His call is preeminent. When that is the case, you will go through fire, you will go through persecution–whatever comes your way–because you know Heaven is on the other side.

When you love God with all of your heart, all of your mind, all of your soul and all of your strength, the only thing that matters is carrying out His mission. You do that with all your might every time you get up, and you do that with joy in your heart because the Father asked you to do it. That's doing the works of Abraham, and that's what God is looking for from Abraham's seed. That's what He wants from you.

You haven't seen any persecution yet. There are still places in the world where you can't preach the Gospel freely without persecution. We rarely think about that because God has blessed us with freedom. I can take you to places in the world where your life is at risk for going through a church door. I've preached to people who had hidden two or three passages of Scripture, and even then they might disappear if God's Word was found. They stood for God. They would witness and minister to people knowing they could die any minute if caught. Those are the seed of Abraham. I pray for those people daily.

> **Hebrews 11:13**
> These all died in faith, not having received the promises, but having seen them afar off, and were persuaded of them, and embraced them, and confessed that they were strangers and pilgrims on the earth.

The Lord showed them that they and their children would not necessarily be the recipients of all the works they were doing for Him. Their ministries were for others. One of the first things that comes to our minds when we minister is, *"What am I going to get out of this?"* These people in the Faith Hall of Fame, however, followed the promises of God even though they weren't going to benefit directly.

When Abraham came to Palestine, he knew he was a stranger and pilgrim in this strange land. He knew it was not where he was raised, but that didn't matter, because following God was about obedience, not his comfort. It was about God's plan. *"For they that say such things declare plainly that they seek a country" (Hebrews 11:14).*

In other words, those who acknowledge that they are strangers and pilgrims on the Earth declare that they seek God's will.

Hebrews 11:15-16
And truly, if they had been mindful of that country from whence they came out, they might have had opportunity to have returned. But now they desire a better country, that is, an heavenly: wherefore God is not ashamed to be called their God: for he hath prepared for them a city.

Abraham could have thought about Ur of Chaldees. He could have looked back to Haran. He could have thought about the past, and if he had, it would have gotten him in trouble. But instead of thinking about where he had come from and what he had left, he looked only forward.

You have to let the past go, whether it's good or bad. If you keep looking backward when you are driving, you're going to run into something. Likewise, when you're walking in faith, you have to look at where you are right now and look ahead to the future that God has promised. When you do so, you will do and have what God said you could do and what you could have. Let the past be the past. The only thing that comes from looking back is trouble. Go forth. God has something wonderful for you. God has a call for you. God has an anointing for you. God has a blessing for you. God has something for you to do if you will let the past go, turn your head around and look to the future.

Be like Abraham and build a tabernacle. Seek the face of God. Find out God's plan for you, and do whatever He gives you to do with all your might and without complaining. Thank God for the honor of being called into His service. It's the highest of honors to serve the true and living God.

2

Doing the Works of Abraham 2.0

We are called to do the works of Abraham, but before we explore those further, let's look at the relationship between faith and works. How was Abraham, a man living under the Old Covenant, declared righteous? In James chapter two we read about Abraham from the pastor of the church at Jerusalem: *"Even so faith, if it hath not works, is dead, being alone" (James 2:17).* The Amplified Bible says: *"So also faith, if it does not have works (deeds and actions of obedience to back it up), by itself is destitute of power [inoperative, dead]" (James 2:17).*

If you really believe, then you will do. James goes on to say: *"Yea, a man may say, Thou hast faith, and I have works: shew me thy faith without thy works, and I will shew thee my faith by my works. Thou believest that there is one God; thou doest well: the devils also believe, and tremble. But wilt thou know, O vain man, that faith*

Not Looking Back

Here's the next one. *"For they that say such things declare plainly that they seek a country. And truly, if they had been mindful of that country from whence they came out, they might have had opportunity to have returned"* (Hebrews 11:14-15). Abraham could have kept looking back, saying, *"I miss Ur of Chaldees."* His wife could have said, *"I miss the shopping in Haran."*

Desiring Heaven

Hebrews 11:16

But now they desire a better country,
that is, an heavenly: wherefore God is
not ashamed to be called their God: for
he hath prepared for them a city.

Every so often you need to hear preaching about Heaven and read the *Book of Revelation* to bring to mind the fact that you were made for eternity. Earth is not your home. *"Blessed is he that readeth, and they that hear the words of this prophecy, and keep those things which are written therein: for the time is at hand"* (Revelation 1:3). Do you know why you're blessed? Because when you finish reading Revelation, you regain a vision and hope for why you're living and where you're going. When you lose the vision for looking for a better place and focus only on the here and now and what's in front of you, you get in trouble.

Receiving the Promises
Hebrews 11:17-19

By faith Abraham, when he was tried, offered up Isaac: and he that had received the promises offered up his only begotten son, Of whom it was said, That in Isaac shall thy seed be called: Accounting that God was able to raise him up, even from the dead; from whence also he received him in a figure.

Because Abraham received the promises, he was willing to go up on the mount and sacrifice the life of his promised son Isaac. *"And he said, Take now thy son, thine only son Isaac, whom thou lovest, and get thee into the land of Moriah; and offer him there for a burnt offering upon one of the mountains which I will tell thee of"* *(Genesis 22:2).*

In short, Abraham and Isaac both obeyed and went to the top of Mount Moriah. Abraham bound his son and was ready to plunge the knife into the chest of his son to offer him as a sacrifice to God Almighty. An angel called out of Heaven and said, *"Hold it!"* Abraham had proven that he was willing to keep his end of the covenant with God. He was willing to offer his only son. When you are in covenant, you do what the other one also is willing to do.

Genesis 22:16-18

And said, By myself have I sworn, saith

the LORD, for because thou hast done
this thing, and hast not withheld thy son,
thine only son: That in blessing I will bless
thee, and in multiplying I will multiply thy
seed as the stars of the heaven, and as
the sand which is upon the sea shore;
and thy seed shall possess the gate of
his enemies; And in thy seed shall all the
nations of the earth be blessed; because thou hast obeyed my voice.

God wasn't identifying general obedience but spe-
cific obedience–being willing to take the life of his son.
"This thing" meant acting on the covenant in Genesis
chapter 17. Because of Abraham's specific obedience,
God promised the following blessings: *"That in blessing
I will bless you."*

God's blessing is an empowerment to prosper in
every area of your life. It is God's power getting involved
in your life, causing you to win regardless of what comes
your way. Genesis chapter 24 said Abraham's life was
blessed in all things–in his body, his money, his family,
his relationships, his standing in the community–all
things. The man was on top.

*"I will multiply thy seed as the stars of the heaven,
and as the sand which is upon the sea shore."* From you
is going to come all of this. Remember how old this man
is? *"Your seed shall possess the gate of his enemies."* In
Hebrew, this means, *"Your seed will drive out the previous tenants and occupy that place."*

"And in thy seed shall all the nations be blessed."
Jesus is the ultimate blessing to all people. He came
through the lineage of Abraham, which is why Jesus
could not have come through the line of Abraham's other
son, Ishmael. Isaac's birthright is legal.

Hebrews 11:17-18
By faith Abraham, when he was tried,
offered up Isaac: and he that had received the promises offered up his only
begotten son, Of whom it was said, That
in Isaac shall thy seed be called.

Abraham had made a decision that the promise was
already enacted. As far as he was concerned–regardless
of what he saw–God's promise was done. In these three
verses, we see that Abraham heard what God told him
to do even though he didn't understand all of it. That
wasn't the first time the Lord had told him about his
seed being numbered with the stars of heaven; the Lord
had told him that in previous encounters. God kept putting the promise in front of Abraham as you should do
everyday by meditating the Word. As far as Abraham
was concerned, Isaac was going to have children, they
were going to have children, and the line would extend
all the way to the Messiah.

Expecting a Miracle

When God told Abraham to take the life of his promised
son, Abraham no doubt wondered what was happening,

but he obeyed anyway since he had received the promise. He knew he was about to see a miracle. He said, *"I'm about to take the life of this boy, and I'm going to watch God raise him from the dead."* Abraham was using his imagination; he could see it in his mind before it happened.

God gave you imagination not so that you could make movies with nine-feet tall blue people in a tree. God gave you imagination so that you could see the promise in advance. When you can see the promise inside first, you will see it on the outside. Seeing it on the inside will cause you to have the hope and motivation to do what's necessary for the promise to come to pass on the outside. An architect can see the building long before the builder ever puts a brick in place. When an architect is done with the plans, he steps back and says, *"That is a masterpiece."*

That's how you need to receive the promises. If you have a financial problem, you need to say, *"My God supplies all my needs according to his riches in glory by Christ Jesus. It's done."* If you have a disease, you need to say, *"He took my infirmities and bore my sicknesses. It's done."* If your life is in danger, you need to say, *"I dwell in the secret places of the most high. God is protecting me. It's done."* You need to receive the promise now. Everybody wants to believe it when it happens, but you need to believe it when God promises.

Abraham is operating in faith, and that's what God likes: *"But without faith it is impossible to please him: for he that cometh to God must believe that he is, and*

that he is a rewarder of them that diligently seek him"
(Hebrews 11:6).

You must believe. This is what God expects. You must believe that He is healer, provider, protector, rewarder and so on. You must keep the vision in front of your face. You must receive the promise.

Jesus said, *"Now if you really are Abraham's seed you will be like him."* Abraham is the measuring stick by which we gauge our faith.

Faith For Life

3

Imitating the Faith Traits of Abraham

Jesus says that if we are Abraham's children, we should imitate his faith, imitate his obedience and imitate his uprightness. To illustrate this, if you listen to my children preach, you'll notice that they sound a lot like me. There are always many similarities between children and their parents. Likewise, if you are Abraham's seed, then you should exhibit some faith traits of Abraham's that excited God. Let's look at some of the traits of Abraham that allowed God to bless him and through his seed bless the entire world.

Having a Family Committed to the Ways of God
Genesis 18:17-19

And the LORD said, Shall I hide from Abraham that thing which I do; Seeing that Abraham shall surely become a great and mighty nation, and all the

> nations of the earth shall be blessed in
> him? For I know him, that he will com-
> mand his children and his household af-
> ter him, and they shall keep the way of
> the LORD, to do justice and judgment;
> that the LORD may bring upon Abra-
> ham that which he hath spoken of him.

God is in covenant with Abraham, and when you are in covenant you are operating in tandem with one another. God says that He knows what Abraham will do; Abraham will make sure his family follows God's way like Abraham does.

When Isaac went up the mountain with his father, he was between the ages of 13 and 32, which means that he was old enough not to let somebody put him on a table to sacrifice. Isaac was willing to put his life on the line for God, too. Abraham's family–his children and his servants–were committed to keeping the way of the Lord. If you stayed in Abraham's house, you had to serve the Lord your God.

You may talk about what God will do for you, but you have to understand that you play a part too. Remember that it took Abraham a while to learn this lesson. Abraham was at least 70 when God first talked to him, and he finally left Haran when he was 75. Years passed before Abraham finally learned his lesson.

Aren't you glad that God has patience with us? I am under construction. If God, the Building Inspector, were to examine my building right now, He would say, *"Here are some defects, Butler."* We are all works in progress.

Commitment is a real problem with believers. When I hear people say that church is too far away, I know that they have commitment issues. They will drive 50 miles to work and then complain about going 15 miles to church. They will go to a football game in the rain, but they won't go to church in the rain. They will sit and watch a movie for three hours but will be wiggling in their seats at church after an hour-and-a-half. These same people want a big commitment from God, however; they want big results with little commitment.

Operating in Faith

Hebrews 11:6

> But without faith it is impossible to please him: for he that cometh to God must believe that he is, and that he is a rewarder of them that diligently seek him.

If you want to please God, you must have faith. If you approach God, you must believe that God is God. He is everything He said. He is everything His name implies. He is healer. He is provider. He is righteousness. He is banker, lawyer, doctor, friend and counselor. Believing He is God and that He is whatever you need is an absolute requirement to having a miracle.

What I am teaching you–how to live by faith–is critical. Inside you is a force of faith. It can get stronger, or it can get weaker. In other words, you believe not only that God is the source that has handled

You may say, *"He was lying."* No, he was simply saying what God said. That's why you have to learn to first find the Gospel. You have to sit under it and have somebody preach it to you. That's why it is important for you to go to church where God's Word is preached. If that's not the case, all you will get is a religious feeling. Your ability to believe, in part, is dependent on where you go to church.

What you say out of your own mouth, to your own self, brings faith or doubt. You can poison yourself or you can build up yourself with your self-talk. Go to the Word and find out what God says about your situation. Don't say what you see. Say what He said.

Calling Forth What God Said

You must be wise in doing so. If your arm is broken and in a cast, and you're dealing with someone who doesn't know the Word and doesn't have insight into what you are doing, don't stand and say, *"I am healed."* They will look at you as if your head is broken, too.

You need to partner with other believers in prayer. You should be able to call up a prayer partner in the church who will say, *"Thank God, healing power will manifest itself in your brain and in your feet and in your ankles and in your stomach and in your blood. Let's praise God today."*

You don't need someone who whines, *"I need faith. I've been through the same thing again and again."* You need somebody who can tell you what the Word says about your condition.

The word *quickeneth* also means *to call forth*. I've been calling forth all kinds of things for a long time. I called my church into existence. This wasn't through my power. No, I just said what God said about it. When God said, *"Go here,"* I started calling and talking about it long before the building and the people were in place.

Getting Hope From God's Word
Romans 4:18

Who against hope believed in hope,
that he might become the father of
many nations, according to that which
was spoken, So shall thy seed be.

This means that all natural hope was gone. There was no way this could ever happen, no way this could be fixed. There was no way this could be resurrected. Where did Abraham get hope?

When we look at biblical characters, we tend to think that these men and women were different than we are. That's why James chapter 5 says that Elijah was a man of like passions as we are. He was up, down, in, out, mad, sad, mean and happy. Yet, he prayed that it wouldn't rain for three years, and it didn't. He prayed again, and it rained. In other words, miracles happened with a man who was just like us. If somebody like me could have manifested miracles in the past through God, I can get it done through God today.

Abraham was just like us, too. He messed up again and again. He disobeyed God in the very beginning. He had problems with lying and stealing. He committed adultery and had a child out of wedlock. He had all kind of problems. But he finally got it together with God, and God made him the most impressive man in the Bible after Jesus. He made him the Father of Faith.

There is hope for you! If God could get that man to that point, God can get you to this point. Where did Abraham find hope?

Romans 15:4
For whatsoever things were written aforetime were written for our learning, that we through patience and comfort of the scriptures might have hope.

Hope comes from the Gospel. You meditate the Word every day because you need hope every day. You need hope before you leave the house, because when you get to work, your coworkers will sap all the hope you have. Not only is Abraham calling things into existence, but also he's sparking his trust and confidence and belief with his mouth, by meditating and thinking about what the Lord said to him.

Meditation on the Word builds a capacity for faith, and meditation on the Word sparks your hope. You need to chew on the Word like you chew on food. You eat two or three times a day because you have a desire for food and you like the taste.

The Word is an acquired taste. When you continue to meditate on the Word and start acting on the Word, you become like David, saying, *"Oh, the Word is good!"* I love the Word!

Romans 8:24

For we are saved by hope: but hope that is seen is not hope: for what a man seeth, why doth he yet hope for?

The word *saved* means *delivered*. You are delivered by hope. *Hope is a confident expectation.* You not only are speaking your future, but also dreaming your future. You are imagining your future. You see yourself with a bouncing baby boy or girl first in your mind, and then in your arms.

This is not easy. You first have to develop yourself along these lines to become proficient. But the Word said, *"The just shall live by faith" (Galatians 3:11).* If you're not living by faith, you're not living the lifestyle of the believer. I didn't say that you would not go to heaven, but you are not an individual who is useful to God. I know that is a tough statement, but it is the truth.

"Who against hope believed in hope, that he might become the father of many nations, according to that which was spoken, So shall thy seed be" (Romans 4:18). Look at the phrase, *"According to that which was spoken."* Abraham's future wasn't just a dream. He wasn't just believing what he wanted to receive. The basis of his faith, just like the basis of your faith, was the Word of God.

being not weak in faith." This verse is an example of strong faith. To see what would have been weak faith, simply drop the word *"not."*

When you are weak in faith, you consider your circumstances now dead. Being weak in faith you consider your marriage now dead. Being weak in faith you consider your financial life now dead. Being weak in faith you consider that there is no way you can be successful. Weak faith considers the present circumstances and talks about those.

Notice that Abraham looked at both his own dead body and that of his wife. You have to look your physical element in the eye. You have to look at your financial element in the eye. You have to look your family element in the eye. To have strong faith, you have to look at whatever it is and speak to it, saying, *"Live!"* Shout at your checkbook and say, *"Live!"* Tell your body, *"You are well."* I have done that in many areas.

Weak faith considers that circumstance. Strong faith considers what God says. The word *consider* means *to look at and think about.* That means you can control your mind and you can control what you think about. In fact, if you meditate on the Word daily, you'll think about that daily.

2 Corinthians 4:16-18

For which cause we faint not; but though our outward man perish, yet the inward man is renewed day by day. For our light affliction, which is but for

a moment, worketh for us a far more
exceeding and eternal weight of glory;
While we look not at the things which
are seen, but at the things which are not
seen: for the things which are seen are
temporal; but the things which are not
seen are eternal.

The words *look not* mean *not focused*. If you're fo-
cusing only on the things that are seen instead of focus-
ing on the goal, then you will speak what you see, not
the goal. And when you speak it, you will have it. It will
affect everything about you, including your emotions
and what will come to pass. Once again, your focus is
vitally important.

Staggering Not at the Promise of God Through Unbelief

Romans 4:20

He staggered not at the promise of God
through unbelief; but was strong in faith,
giving glory to God.

In other words, Abraham didn't say, *"This is too
big."* The word staggered means to withdraw. He didn't
withdraw from the promise even though he looked at his
body and he looked at his wife. He looked at experience;
he didn't know anyone else who had ever had a child at
his age. He didn't stagger even though he couldn't find
anybody else that would agree with him. In other words,

the only thing Abraham had going for him was the fact that he had a Word from God and decided it was stronger and more powerful and more real than all of his experience. That only happens by a decision.

When I am teaching the Scriptures, you may think, *"Does God really expect me to do this."* Yes, God does expect that of you. He said if you are Abraham's seed you will do the works of Abraham. You will follow the faith of Abraham. *Hebrews 6:12* says that those who received the promise are those who walk in faith with patience like Abraham. You can receive every promise of God. To do so, you can't say, *"I want it and I want it now."* You, too, must wait on God's timing.

Giving Glory to God

When it feels like you're failing and when everybody else is telling you that you're failing, you respond by giving God glory and praise. People will think you're crazy. When you should be crying, you're rejoicing.

Instead of talking about how bad it is, you are talking about how good it is. You are exercising faith, and those who have been declared righteous live this way, day in and day out, not only in an emergency.

To live this way requires a complete renewing of the mind and a complete change of the way you've been thinking. It requires a whole different approach to life.

Being Fully Persuaded
Romans 4:21

And being fully persuaded that, what

he had promised, he was able also to
perform.

How in the world do you go from looking at your situation to being fully persuaded? Again, don't forget that
when Abraham started out he was a moon worshipper.
He lied, he was an adulterer, and he was full of doubts.
He went from that to being fully persuaded. Abraham
wasn't a supernatural man. He got happy, sad, encour-
aged and depressed like we do. This means that every
one of you can live by faith. Every one of you can have
God's miracles manifest in your life if you do what Abraham did. You can bring to life whatever is dead in your
life and change it through the power of the living God.

You can't listen to bad news and believe it. There
is going to be a negative report in your life all the time.
Whose report do you choose to believe? God said you are
an overcomer. Others say you are a loser. God said, *"I
am the way."* Others say there's no way. God said that
He supplies all your needs. Others say you can't make it
in this economy. Whose report do you choose to believe?

Romans 4:22-25

And therefore it was imputed to him for
righteousness. Now it was not written for
his sake alone, that it was imputed to
him;

But for us also, to whom it shall be imputed, if we believe on him that raised

from that son would be as the sand of the seashore. God promised that the blessing would operate in every area of his life, that he would be blessed coming in and going out. God showed him the future, even the ministry of the Lord Jesus. God revealed Himself to Abraham, and Abraham was able to have all that God promised because he operated in confident expectation or hope. Abraham operated in faith, and he learned how to be constant, steadfast and unmovable. Patience became a force in his life.

Hebrews 6:15-16

And so, after he had patiently endured, he obtained the promise. For men verily swear by the greater: and an oath for confirmation is to them an end of all strife.

In biblical times, if a man gave an oath and swore with a blood covenant, he could be killed if he didn't keep his promise.

Hebrews 6:17-18

Wherein God, willing more abundantly to shew unto the heirs of promise the immutability of his counsel, confirmed it by an oath:

That by two immutable things, in which it was impossible for God to lie, we might

have a strong consolation, who have
fled for refuge to lay hold upon the
hope set before us.

God confirmed His promise by an oath because He
wanted to show His immutability to the heirs of the
promise. In other words, God wants you to know that
when He says something, He doesn't change His mind.
When He says something, it's going to happen. He
wants you to know that He will do what He says He will
do. If you can find a promise in His Word, you can stand
on it until the day you take your last breath. When
you get to Heaven, you will find that His promise still
stands.

God confirmed the immutability of His counsel by
an oath that you and I could see. The two things that
God showed us are the beating of Jesus' body and the
shedding of Jesus' blood. In other words, God said, *"I
backed up what I said I was going to do for Abraham
and Abraham's seed. I kept my end of the promise. When
Abraham offered up his only son, I offered up my only
Son. Abraham was willing to shed his son's blood, and
I shed my Son's blood. You should have strong comfort
because now you know that my power is fully available
for every promise in my Word."*

God is behind His Word, and if you place yourself
on His Word and do what His Word says, you have God
as your power source. There has never been anyone
or anything big enough or strong enough to withstand
Him.

Living With Hope

Since God is unchangeable, not only do we know what happened in the past, but also we have an expectation of the wonderful things that will happen.

Hebrews 6:19-20
Which hope we have as an anchor of the soul, both sure and stedfast, and which entereth into that within the veil; Whither the forerunner is for us entered, even Jesus, made an high priest for ever after the order of Melchisedec.

An anchor keeps a ship from floating away with the current. This hope keeps you steadfast. This hope helps your soul, which is your mind, will and emotions. This anchor keeps you from being depressed, sad or angry.

Remember, there was a veil in the Holies of Holies between the Holy Place and the Most Holy place in the temple in Jerusalem. For a time, God's Spirit resided only in there. But there was a veil also in Heaven. Jesus, the forerunner–Someone who entered before you–took His blood and went through the veil in Heaven. He went to the seat of mercy in front of God the Father, placed His blood on that seat, and declared that you were innocent of all charges.

Thus, the hope that keeps our anchor steadfast is the knowledge that if we do what God says, we are going to Heaven to be with Him throughout all eternity. Heaven is a real place. People live, work and have fun there.

In Heaven, you won't be an oversized baby with wings on your back. No. Read the *Book of Revelation*. The New Jerusalem is there, a city 144,000 miles high, long, deep and wide with twelve entrances, each of which is several miles long and high. There's a river flowing, and trees with abundant fruit. The streets are made out of gold.

Holding the expectation of eternity in Heaven in front of you keeps you from getting stupid, thinking only about what is happening here on Earth for a very small amount of time. Nothing–fame, fortune, houses and lands, status–absolutely nothing is worth losing Heaven over.

Abraham lived with an expectation of Heaven. He walked 400 miles on foot–from Ur of the Chaldees all the way to the Promised Land–on the strength of that hope. He started all over in his seventies, living in tents. He did that because God placed a vision in his heart.

Proverbs 13:12
Hope deferred **[removed or delayed]** maketh the heart sick **[weak and wounded]**: but when the desire cometh, it is a tree of life.

Your hope can be set aside, and depression follows that. But hope realized gives life.

Romans 15:4
For whatsoever things were written aforetime were written for our learning,

people don't know anything about faith and don't live by faith. They only use faith in an emergency; they use faith as a "Get-Out-of-Jail-Free" card. But if you are supposed to live by your faith, as God said, then you must be able to live that way purposefully. Those who live by faith are folks who win.

Hearing God is a prerequisite to living by faith. If you can't hear what God is saying to you, then you can't live by faith. Calling forth those things that you don't see as though they have already happened is a prerequisite of living by faith. Faith doesn't call what it sees; faith calls what it believes and what it wants to see. Faith doesn't talk about the problem; it talks about the solution. Many Christians talk about the problem. They look at the bills and talk about them; they look at the doctor's report and talk about that. None of that is living by faith, and God operates with you only by faith.

The Speaking God

Why is it a hard thing for people to believe that God would speak to somebody? If an engineer at Ford Motor Company can create a car that will respond to your words, why would anyone doubt that God can speak to anybody? The creation is not smarter than the Creator.

Acts 22:10
And I said, What shall I do, LORD? And the Lord said unto me, Arise, and go into Damascus; and there it shall be told

thee of all things which are appointed
for thee to do.

You see a couple of things in this verse. First, you
see God speaking to a man, Paul. Then God tells him
that if he goes where God tells him to go, He will tell
him the next step. Many people don't like that, saying,
*"Lord, why don't you just tell me the whole plan so I can
consider whether or not I want to do this?"* If you could
see the whole picture, there would not be a requirement
of faith. God wants His children to operate in faith, just
as you want your children to operate in faith. You want
them to trust you so much that they respond to your
word.

God loves it when all the evidence and everybody
else say something different, but you say, *"God said it."*
He has every right to expect that from you. God had His
Son die, go to hell in your place and rise from the dead—
all for you. You ought to be willing to say, *"If He said it,
that settles it."* God has no right to expect that out of you
unless He is willing to give you a Word.

The Holy Ghost spoke in *Acts chapter 13,* giving
instructions for Barnabas and Saul's ministerial call.

Acts 13:1-2
Now there were in the church that was
at Antioch certain prophets and teachers; as Barnabas, and Simeon that was
called Niger, and Lucius of Cyrene, and
Manaen, which had been brought up

God–so shall thy seed be–and that's the reason he could become strong in faith and give glory to God. If hearing from God is of critical importance in having faith, then we better learn how to hear the voice of God. We better know how to get that Word from God.

First John 5:7 says that there are *"three that bare record in heaven: the Father, the Word and the Spirit."* These three are one in name, purpose, thought and direction. There isn't any disagreement between the Father, the Son and the Holy Ghost. It is the triune God. If one says something, the other two are in agreement.

You may say, *"Well, you never know what God is going to do."* God, however, wants you to know what He is going to do because you are His children. He doesn't want Satan's children to know what is going on; He wants you to know what is going on because you are His.

Christianity is not a religion. It is an experience with Somebody who is alive, Somebody who wants to give you direction, Somebody who will change your life. *His name is Jesus Christ, the Messiah.* You need to spend time with Him and the Holy Spirit on a daily basis. Many people say, *"I'm getting the kids together; I don't have time."* Or, *"I have to be at the job, and I don't have time."* Or, *"I stayed up until two a.m. watching a movie, and I'm too tired to get up early to spend time with God."* Those are all just excuses. You will always find a way to do what you really want to do.

If you make a decision to grow in the things of God on a daily basis, you will be a person who is far more perceptive spiritually than someone trying to hear God in the middle of a storm. It is not impossible to build a house in the middle of a storm, but it's a lot easier to build it when things are calm. The time to develop yourself is while things are working well and while you are healthy and healed.

People want to run to God when trouble comes, but it's far better to live by the following four things on a daily basis:

You live by faith: Romans 1:17
For therein is the righteousness of God revealed from faith to faith: as it is written, The just shall live by faith.

You live by the Word: Matthew 4:4
But he answered and said, It is written, Man shall not live by bread alone, but by every word that proceedeth out of the mouth of God.

You live through the Spirit: Galatians 5:25
If we live in the Spirit, let us also walk in the Spirit.

You live in the Spirit: Acts 17:28
For in him we live, and move, and have our being; as certain also of your own poets have said, For we are also his offspring.

Hearing the Voice of God

od is not your enemy. God is your friend. He's your Father. He lives in you, and He wants to speak to you! As we have seen, hearing God speak is an essential component to living by faith. In this chapter, I am going to explore the seven ways that you can hear the voice of God.

Number 1: Hearing the Voice of God Through the Written Word

Matthew 4:4 says, *"Man shall not live by bread alone, but by every word that proceedeth out of the mouth of God."* What does it mean to live by the Word? It means that in every decision you make, the Word is God's voice. The Word is God speaking to you. The Word decides all decisions. My wife and I rarely disagree, but when we do, she and I both go to the Word to find out what it says about the subject of our disagreement. The

Word solves our arguments. Every time that we do that, we find out that both of us were wrong, and we apologize to one another and walk in love.

Living by the Word means that you go to the Word about your financial decisions. The Word tells you how to structure your finances. The Word tells you not to load up with debt. The Word tells you to be generous with others. You don't need a voice from Heaven. You have the Word!

Hearing the voice of God doesn't happen by accident. You have to be deliberate about spending time in the Word, finding out what the Word says about every sector of your life, and then living by that. God is smarter than you are. Peter talks about the importance of this.

2 Peter 1:15
Moreover I will endeavour that ye may
be able after my decease to have
these things always in remembrance.

"*I taught you this,*" Peter said. "*Remember. Don't forget. For we have not followed cunningly devised fables, when we made known unto you the power and coming of our Lord Jesus Christ, but were eyewitnesses of his majesty*" (*2 Peter 1:16*). In other words, Peter said, "*I was there. I saw this with my eyes.*"

2 Peter 1:17-19
For he received from God the Father honour and glory, when there came such a voice to him from the excellent glory, This is my beloved Son, in whom I am well pleased. And this voice which came from heaven we heard, when we were with him in the holy mount.

We have also a more sure word of prophecy; whereunto ye do well that ye take heed, as unto a light that shineth in a dark place, until the day dawn and the day star arise in your hearts.

In other words, what we have is more real and more sure than what we see with our eyes and hear with our ears. If it were dark outside and you turned off all the lights, you would be in a dark room. If you struck a match, your eyes would rivet to the light. There's a single focus to the light.

It is dark before morning, before the day star arises. The day star is the sun, and it will rise in your heart! It will rise in your emotions, your visions and your feelings. When the sun begins to rise from the East, it gets lighter and lighter until there is no more darkness. Peter is saying, *"Stay riveted to the Word, the more sure Word of prophecy. It will get lighter and lighter until there will be no more darkness at all–no more poverty, no more depression, no more fear, no more sickness, and no more lack."* This is the power of the voice of God, the Word. *"Knowing this first, that no prophecy of the scripture is of any private interpretation. For the prophecy came not in old time by the will of man: but holy men of God spake as they were moved by the Holy Ghost"* (2 Peter 1:20-21).

The anointing came on holy men, and the Spirit of God utilized them to pen the Bible, each and every word. This is not a private interpretation. The Word is for everyone; anyone can get revelation. The only reason people don't get revelation is because they choose to do something other than hear the Word, read and meditate on the Word and ask the Holy Ghost for revelation.

Number 2: Hearing the Voice of God Through an Inward Witness

1 John 5:6

This is he that came by water and blood, even Jesus Christ; not by water only, but by water and blood. And it is the Spirit that beareth witness, because the Spirit is truth.

The Holy Spirit is the One who bears *witness*, a word that means *evidence*. The Holy Spirit is evidence, a witness, to you. Remember that you are not a body and you are not a soul. You live inside a physical body, but you are a spirit being that has a soul, which is inclusive of your mind, will and emotions. You are tri-part—spirit, soul and body—just as God is a trinity: Father, Son and

Holy Ghost. The Holy Spirit dwells in the real you, and He will surround all facets of you if allowed.

> ### 1 John 5:7-10
> For there are three that bear record in heaven, the Father, the Word, and the Holy Ghost: and these three are one. And there are three that bear witness in earth, the Spirit, and the water, and the blood: and these three agree in one. If we receive the witness of men, the witness of God is greater: for this is the witness of God which he hath testified of his Son. He that believeth on the Son of God hath the witness in himself: he that believeth not God hath made him a liar; because he believeth not the record that God gave of his Son.

You know when you are hearing truth. You need to slow down and learn to listen. You can shrug if off, but the truth bears witness. Romans chapter one says that those with reprobate minds are those who once knew God, both by nature and by the witness in themselves. Even the sinner knows God is there. He just refuses to acknowledge Him as God and obey the truth.

Growing in those seven things that you need to do every morning helps you hear God. Too many people want to spend a short time on the things of God. They become a believer and then expect things to happen quickly. Wait! They perfected their messed up state; they developed and grew in habits that produced the problems. They can't just dab a little bit in the things of God and expect something to happen. People say, *"I am doing everything that God tells me to do, so I guess it doesn't work."* It works if you spend time hearing God and growing in the things of God.

Let's look at an example of the inward witness in Acts chapter 27. Paul is in a real life situation. He is about to go on a trip.

Acts 27:6-10
And there the centurion found a ship of Alexandria sailing into Italy; and he put us therein.

And when we had sailed slowly many days, and scarce were come over against Cnidus, the wind not suffering us, we sailed under Crete, over against Salmone; And, hardly passing it, came unto a place which is called The fair havens; nigh whereunto was the city of Lasea.

Now when much time was spent, and when sailing was now dangerous, because the fast was now already past, Paul admonished them, And said unto them, Sirs, I perceive that this voyage

will be with hurt and much damage, not
only of the lading and ship, but also of
our lives.

The phrase *"I perceive"* meant that he had a witness. The Spirit of God was showing him these things
in order to save his life and the lives of the people who
were with him. How do you know it's the Spirit speaking
to you?

2 Corinthians 5:17
Therefore if any man be in Christ, he is a
new creature **[creation]**: old things are
passed away; behold **[look]**, all things
are become new.

All means *everything.* All things are new. You no
longer have your old, demonic nature. You are not a
spiritual schizophrenic, with God and the devil warring
against one another inside of you. A Christian cannot
be possessed with a demon spirit. You may have one on
your body messing with you, but that is outside you. The
devil is not a match for the Holy Ghost. They are not
fighting to see which one is going to win.

I have experienced numerous situations where I
was about to die, but my life was saved because I heard
the Holy Spirit. One time, the Spirit of God spoke to
me early in the morning before I boarded a commercial
flight. He told me not to get on that airplane, just as he
spoke to Paul. I called my secretary and told her to can-

cel my flight. That flight crashed a hundred miles south of Detroit and killed more than 200 people. God saved me. He wasn't just trying to save me; I know He had tried to speak to the other people on that plane, also. He didn't let that happen; they did. If I hadn't listened to the Spirit, I wouldn't be here today.

> **Acts 27:14-19**
> But not long after there arose against it a tempestuous wind, called Euroclydon. And when the ship was caught, and could not bear up into the wind, we let her drive. And running under a certain island which is called Clauda, we had much work to come by the boat:
>
> Which when they had taken up, they used helps, undergirding the ship; and, fearing lest they should fall into the quicksands, strake sail, and so were driven.
>
> And we being exceedingly tossed with a tempest, the next day they lightened the ship; And the third day we cast out with our own hands the tackling of the ship.

In other words, they let the ship go wherever it was going to take them. They stopped trying to fight it. They threw out everything that was on the boat. That cargo cost people money. Not listening to the Holy Ghost is how you lose houses, cars and money. Remember, the Spirit had showed Paul all of this *before* they ever set sail, but the people didn't listen. He was a prisoner, so he had to go.

> **Acts 27:20**
> And when neither sun nor stars in many days appeared, and no small tempest lay on us, all hope that we should be saved was then taken away.

They were in the middle of a hurricane and were in total darkness for days and days. I want you to visualize what was happening. They were in a terrible situation.

> **Acts 27:21-25**
> But after long abstinence Paul stood forth in the midst of them, and said, Sirs, ye should have hearkened unto me, and not have loosed from Crete, and to have gained this harm and loss. And now I exhort you to be of good cheer: for there shall be no loss of any man's life among you, but of the ship. **[This ship belonged to somebody and cost a lot of money.]**

> For there stood by me this night the
> angel of God, whose I am, and whom I
> serve, Saying, Fear not, Paul; thou must
> be brought before Caesar: and, lo, God
> hath given thee all them that sail with
> thee. Wherefore, sirs, be of good cheer:
> for I believe God, that it shall be even as
> it was told me.

I don't think anybody would have to tell you what to do in a situation like that. You would be praying! Paul was praying all that time, and another word from God came. Faith comes by hearing a word of God. When that word came and told Paul that no one was going to die, Paul said, *"Let's be of good cheer! We're going to lose a ship, but we can get another ship. We've lost the cargo, but we can get other cargo."* Paul believed God!

You may lose your house, your car, your clothes and everything else, but you can get more of that. You can't get another life. Paul said to the centurion and to the soldiers, *"Except these abide in the ship, ye cannot be saved"* (Acts 27:31).

This time, they listened to him: *"Wherefore I pray you to take some meat: for this is for your health: for there shall not an hair fall from the head of any of you.*

And when he had thus spoken, he took bread, and gave thanks to God in presence of them all: and when he had broken it, he began to eat" (Acts 27:34-35).

Remember, they'd been in a hurricane for fourteen days. After Paul had spoken, he took bread and gave thanks. Paul was giving thanks that they were going to live; he was giving thanks that he had received a word from God. They were of good cheer, even though they were still in the storm! What you do affects everybody around you.

Acts 27:37
And we were in all in the ship two hundred threescore and sixteen souls.

The boat finally broke apart, but every single one of them made it to shore. While they were sitting around a fire warming themselves, a viper came and fastened itself on Paul's hand. He shook off the viper into the fire.

That is what you have to do in life. You have to shake off your problems. God told him he was going to live and not die. God told him he was going to Caesar. That word from God gave him faith. That word from God determined how he acted.

Number 3: Hearing the Voice of God Through the Voice of the Holy Spirit

In Acts chapter 10, Peter was on a house top, and he decided to skip a meal and spend a little time with God in prayer. There's not a requirement about fasting from food in the New Testament; you don't move the hand of God because you don't eat. Fasting is not for God's benefit. Fasting is for your benefit. When you fast, all that time you would have spent preparing the meal, eating and cleaning up is spent in the Word and in prayer.

That extra time with God sharpens you spiritually. The more time you spend with God, the greater opportunity you will have to hear from Him.

> **Acts 10:9-14**
> On the morrow, as they went on their journey, and drew nigh unto the city, Peter went up upon the housetop to pray about the sixth hour: And he became very hungry, and would have eaten: but while they made ready, he fell into a trance, And saw heaven opened, and a certain vessel descending upon him, as it had been a great sheet knit at the four corners, and let down to the earth:
>
> Wherein were all manner of four footed beasts of the earth, and wild beasts, and creeping things, and fowls of the air. And there came a voice to him, Rise, Peter; kill, and eat. But Peter said, Not so, Lord; for I have never eaten any thing that is common or unclean.

First, Peter recognized who was speaking to him. He didn't ask, *"Who is that?"* You may say, *"How do I know the difference between God's voice, the devil's voice and my own voice?"* My parishioners know my voice. If they were in a crowd somewhere and heard my voice, they would know that it was Bishop. I could be with thousands of people, and if my wife said something, I'd know it was her immediately. How? I've been with her for 35+ years; I know her voice. **The more time you spend with God, the easier it is for you to recognize His voice and to know that God is speaking to you.**

Acts 10:15-19

And the voice spake unto him again the second time, What God hath cleansed, that call not thou common. This was done thrice: and the vessel was received up again into heaven.

Now while Peter doubted in himself what this vision which he had seen should mean, behold, the men which were sent from Cornelius had made enquiry for Simon's house, and stood before the gate, And called, and asked whether Simon, which was surnamed Peter, were lodged there. While Peter thought on the vision, the Spirit said unto him, Behold, three men seek thee.

The capital "S" refers to the Holy Spirit. Once again, the Holy Spirit is on the inside of believers. Peter hears that voice on the inside, *not with his physical ears.* What did the Spirit say? The Lord was introduc-

what's in the Bible. If you heard what you thought was a word from the Holy Ghost and He told you, *"Go ahead and divorce your wife and marry this woman half your age,"* that wasn't the Holy Ghost talking. A voice may have been speaking, but it wasn't the Holy One. Don't confuse what you want to do with what the Holy Ghost is saying. Anything the Lord says to you will line up with the Scripture. If you can't find some Scripture for it, then you need to forget what you heard.

Acts 13:1-2
Now there were in the church that was at Antioch certain prophets and teachers; as Barnabas, and Simeon that was called Niger, and Lucius of Cyrene, and Manaen, which had been brought up with Herod the tetrarch, and Saul. As they ministered to the Lord, and fasted, the Holy Ghost said, Separate me Barnabas and Saul for the work whereunto I have called them.

There are several things in this verse that you need to know. If you are going to do anything in ministry, God will separate you. You can't be in the ministry and live like the world, talk like the world, and act like the world. You must be separate. There's a price you pay in ministry. You don't get to do what everybody else gets to do.

Later in Acts chapter 13, Paul and Barnabas were

in the ministry–Paul was a Bible teacher–but now God was going to separate him into the office of an apostle, a sent one, particularly to plant churches in Gentile areas and raise up people in the Kingdom and Gospel of Lord.

The Holy Ghost will speak to you and give instruction that way. I don't know how many times I have had the Holy Spirit deal that way with me: *"And when they had fasted and prayed, and laid their hands on them, they sent them away. So they, being sent forth by the Holy Ghost, departed unto Seleucia; and from thence they sailed to Cyprus" (Acts 13:3-4).* The Holy Ghost spoke, telling them where to go. He'll do the same thing for you.

Number 4: Hearing the Voice of God Through Preaching and Teaching

Let's look at an extended passage of Scripture: *"But what saith it? The word is nigh thee, even in thy mouth, and in thy heart: that is, the word of faith, which we preach; That if thou shalt confess with thy mouth the Lord Jesus, and shalt believe in thine heart that God hath raised him from the dead, thou shalt be saved.*

For with the heart man believeth unto righteousness; and with the mouth confession is made unto salvation **[deliverance, health, safety, soundness, and healing].**

For the scripture saith, Whosoever believeth on him shall not be ashamed. For there is no difference between the Jew and the Greek: for the same Lord over all is rich unto all that call upon him. For whosoever shall call

*upon the name of the Lord shall be saved. How then
shall they call on him in whom they have not believed?
and how shall they believe in him of whom they have not
heard? and how shall they hear without a preacher? And
how shall they preach, except they be sent? as it is written, How beautiful are the feet of them that preach the
gospel of peace, and bring glad tidings of good things!*

*But they have not all obeyed the gospel. For Esaias
saith, Lord, who hath believed our report? So then faith
cometh by hearing, and hearing by the word of God"*
(Romans 10:8-17).

God speaks to you through preaching and teaching
of the Word. When a minister is preaching, the Holy
Ghost speaks more than just what that preacher says.
In all the years I have been in the ministry, I can't tell
you the countless times I've had someone write me a let-
ter, testify or come and tell me how God spoke to them
about something I didn't even mention in my sermon. In
other words, every time that you come to hear the Word
taught and preached you ought to come with your heart
open, even if you think you know the message. Why? Because the Holy Ghost will say more than what you hear
with your physical ears. The Lord will speak to you.

One time I was at a ministers' convention, and I
already knew what the minister was preaching. I knew
the Scriptures, and I knew how he was approaching
them, but the Holy Ghost started beating me up with
his Words. The Lord can illuminate His Word if you
have ears to hear. *As a listener, you should not be personality specific; you should be Word of God specific.*

Even more, you ought to be Holy Ghost specific. You should come expecting the Lord to give you a great revelation from God, regardless of who is speaking.

Paul faced the issue of people being personality specific. There was a schism in Corinth. Some people liked Paul, and others liked Apollos. Paul said, *"Who is Paul, Apollos and Peter? They're nobody, just people whom God has called."*

It's all about the Holy Ghost, and when you are open to the Holy Ghost, He will speak to you, even though it may not be what you want to hear.

Just because someone is sitting in church doesn't mean that the person is hearing from the Holy Ghost. An individual hungry for God can go to church, thinking, *"I am open to what the Lord is trying to say to me today,"* and God can give him a revelation that can change his life forever. The person sitting next to him can hear the same Word in the same place from the same person and say, *"Nothing happened here today."*

Another person can be in the same place and have a manifest healing. It all has to do with person and his or her expectations. People go to church for a lot of reasons—out of religious habit, an attempt to network, looking for a spouse or for entertainment. All of those reasons mean you won't get much out of it.

You should not deprive yourself of opportunities for God to speak to you about how to live. You need more revelation, understanding and feeding from the Word of God than you can receive by going to church only once a week. If you ate only once a week, you wouldn't be very strong. The reason there are so many weak Christians is that they eat the Word too infrequently.

Acts 16:6
Now when they had gone throughout Phrygia and the region of Galatia, and were forbidden of the Holy Ghost to preach the word in Asia.

Paul was forbidden to preach the Word in Asia. *"Doesn't the Bible say to go out into all the world and preach the Gospel to every creature?"* Yes, this is Jesus' general command to the church, but as an individual you need to find out what part of the world and what creatures He has assigned you. You can't be everywhere at once. If I am in Texas, it is because the Holy Ghost gave me an assignment to be there. If I were in California, nothing would be happening, because God had not sent me.

Most ministers never get past the first stage of their ministry. I knew when I was nineteen years old that I was going to find out what God said and I wasn't going anywhere until I did. Scripture doesn't tell you where to go, but God leads people to specific places. If you say, *"Lord I will do whatever you tell me to do,"* then you better spend time in prayer so He can tell you what to do. The blessing comes when you are where you are supposed to be.

Acts 16:7

After they were come to Mysia, they assayed to go into Bithynia: but the Spirit suffered them not.

The Holy Spirit not only told them where to go, but also told them where not to go. Most ministers fail because of what happens after they are called. They don't find out exactly where they are supposed to be and they don't find out exactly what they are supposed to do. They don't obey precisely what they are told to do. They follow other people's methodologies instead of finding out what the Lord has specifically for them.

God told you to be led by His Spirit. He told you to obey Him. If you are not led by His Spirit and you don't obey Him—if you are in the wrong place at the wrong time and you get beat up—don't blame God. Don't say, *"Why did God allow this to happen to me?"* It wasn't God who allowed it to happen to you; it was you who allowed it happen to you. Before you can you use your faith to get out of the mess you find yourself in, you have to acknowledge your sin. Sin is missing the mark. *First John 1:9* was not written to sinners; it was written to Christians: *"my little children."* If you acknowledge your sin, God is faithful and just to forgive you and cleanse you from all of our unrighteousness. Stop blaming God, and stop blaming other people.

8

Hearing the Voice of God 2.0

In the last chapter, we looked at four of the ways that you can hear the voice of God: through the written Word, through an inward witness, through the voice of the Holy Spirit, and through preaching and teaching of the Word. Once again, developing the capacity to hear God and receive direction and guidance will be the key to living as an overcomer, even more so as we get closer to the coming of Jesus Christ. Let's go on to explore three more ways that you can hear God speak to you.

Number 5: Hearing the Voice of God Through Visions and Dreams

"And they passing by Mysia came down to Troas. And a vision appeared to Paul in the night; There stood a man of Macedonia, and prayed him, saying, Come over into Macedonia, and help us. And after he had seen the vision, immediately we endeavoured to go into Macedonia,

assuredly gathering that the Lord had called us for to preach the gospel unto them" (Acts 16:8-10).

Don't get me wrong. I don't want you running after voices; health officials might lock you up and put you in one of those jackets. God is not speaking to you every time you have a dream or a vision. No, you might have just eaten too much pizza.

There are multiple checks and balances when God speaks to you. *First,* there is going to be something of God about it. *Second,* it will line up with the Scriptures. *Third,* there will be a witness about it. *Lastly,* you will get God's results from responding to a vision from Him.

Obeying God doesn't necessarily mean you are going to have smooth sailing all the time. In Acts chapter 16, Paul and Silas were ministering in Macedonia as a result of being called there in a vision. Remember, they had wanted to go to Asia, but God had said, *"No, go over here."* It wasn't the Lord's will that they were beaten. Jesus said Satan comes immediately to steal the Word that was sown (*Mark 4*).

Satan immediately attacked them because they were in the will of God. They stayed in faith. They knew God sent them; the attack didn't throw them off course because they had heard from God. If you don't know that you have a Word from God, when something hard hits you, you will quit. You will run off. You will blame God. You will do something in the flesh and mess the whole thing up.

Doing the will of God doesn't mean that you won't get attacked; it just means that you will win. But if you're not in the will of God and you get attacked, you will lose.

Paul and Silas were pulled into the public square, stripped of their clothes, beaten and thrown in prison. Their feet and ankles were fastened in stocks. Look at how Paul and Silas responded to this: *"Who, having received such a charge, thrust them into the inner prison, and made their feet fast in the stocks. And at midnight Paul and Silas prayed, and sang praises unto God: and the prisoners heard them" (Acts 16:24-25).*

Do you think they prayed, *"Lord why did you lead us here? Lord, we did what you told us to do, and we were beaten and thrown into prison."* No, I think they prayed, *"Lord you told us to come here, and Satan saw us coming and being effective for the kingdom of God. He attacked us. Thank you for the honor and glory of being called. We want you to know that we will stand for you whatever you call us to do."*

Whatever prayer they prayed, it made them start giving God praise and glory. Whatever has happened to you, begin your prayer with *"Hallelujah"* and thank God that His mercy endures forever. The Lord is on your side. Paul and Silas sang praises to God so loudly that the whole jail heard them praise.

Look at how the next verse begins: *"And suddenly there was a great earthquake, so that the foundations of the prison were shaken: and immediately all the doors were opened, and every one's bands were loosed" (Acts 16:26).*

That's the way God moves–suddenly. Things are one way this moment, but the next second everything is changed. Suddenly a great earthquake came and shook the prison doors, and their jail door was opened. If you want to have miracles like Abraham and like Paul, find the will of God and set your faith. Determine not to be deterred by whatever attack the enemy brings your way. Walk by faith and not by sight, and you will have a *"suddenly."* Suddenly you will be healed. Suddenly you will be delivered. Suddenly you will be set free. Suddenly you will see the move of God.

The jail door opened for Paul and Silas. Most people would have said, *"Thank you, Lord,"* and run out of that jail. Not Paul and Silas. That door opened and the jailer, thinking that the prisoners had escaped, was ready to kill himself. Paul said, *"We aren't going anywhere. We are staying here."* When God moves, everybody hangs around to see what is going to happen. Paul preached another famous sermon: *"Believe on the Lord Jesus Christ, and thou shalt be saved, and thy house"* (verse 31).

The jailer got saved, his house got saved and Paul built the church right there. He had a miracle of God. But it started with hearing. It started with a specific word. It started with following.

You can't just say, *"I believe, I believe, I believe,"* and then go out and borrow the money and call it faith. You can't accumulate all that debt and when the value drops thirty percent, say, *"Why did God let this happen to me?"* It wasn't God at all.

There's a difference between mercy and justice. Justice is when you get what you deserve. Mercy is when you receive grace that you don't deserve. If you will come to Him, acknowledge your failures, and make the decision to hear and see what He is telling you, then He can reverse your situation suddenly. But He will say, *"Don't go back and sin again."*

Number 6: Hearing the Voice of God Through Prophetic Utterance

1 Corinthians 14:24-25, 29

But if all prophesy, and there come in one that believeth not, or one unlearned, he is convinced of all, he is judged of all: And thus are the secrets of his heart made manifest; and so falling down on his face he will worship God, and report that God is in you of a truth. Let the prophets speak two or three, and let the other judge.

Don't miss the phrase, *"and let the other judge."* The Lord could speak to you through a prophet's ministry, but any time you hear God through a vessel like that, it must be judged by several criteria.

Criteria number one: *"Is this the first time you have heard this?"* God's gifts are perfect, but the vessels that He uses are imperfect.

If it is new to you and God has never witnessed to you about this before, then set this prophecy on a shelf and allow the Lord to confirm it with other things.

Criteria number two: *"Does it line up with the Word?"*

Criteria number three: *"Does your spiritual authority–your pastor or someone over you–confirm this message?"* A man of God recently prophesied to me about things God had already spoken to me about. I already knew everything he said, and I didn't ask God for confirmation, but He gave it to me anyway. That is the proper use of the prophet's office, and I received it. While it wasn't new to me, it confirmed what God had already told me, and it motivated me all the more to establish works in different cities.

"Peter therefore was kept in prison, but prayer was made without ceasing of the church unto God for him. And when Herod would have brought him forth, the same night Peter was sleeping between two soldiers, bound with two chains: and the keepers before the door kept the prison" (Acts 12:5-6).

Peter was in prison. Not only was he facing the pressure of a scheduled execution, but also somebody he knew had been killed by Herod a few days before. If you had been in this position–bound with chains between two soldiers–do you think you would have been sleeping? Why was Peter so confident?

2 Peter 1:16
For we have not followed cunningly devised fables, when we made known unto you the power and coming of our

Lord Jesus Christ, but were eyewitnesses
of his majesty.

Peter had experienced the glory and power of God
in Jesus Christ firsthand: *"For he received from God the
Father honour and glory, when there came such a voice
to him from the excellent glory, This is my beloved Son,
in whom I am well pleased. And this voice which came
from heaven we heard, when we were with him in the
holy mount.*

*We have also a more sure word of prophecy; where-
unto ye do well that ye take heed, as unto a light that
shineth in a dark place, until the day dawn, and the
day star arise in your hearts: Knowing this first, that no
prophecy of the scripture is of any private interpretation.*

*For the prophecy came not in old time by the will of
man: but holy men of God spake as they were moved by
the Holy Ghost" (2 Peter 1:17-21).*

Hearing from God is not just for apostles, prophets,
evangelists, pastors and teachers; it is for anyone who
seeks a Word from God. Jesus had already told Peter
what he was going to minister and how he was going
to die. He had already received a word from God, so he
knew he was not dying in that prison. A word from God
will cause you to be able to stay in faith. A word from
God will cause you to be able to defeat whatever trap
the enemy has set for you. A word from God will get you
through any difficult situation.

Number 7: Hearing the Voice of God Through the Ministry of Angels
Acts 12:6-7
And when Herod would have brought him forth, the same night Peter was sleeping between two soldiers, bound with two chains: and the keepers before the door kept the prison. And, behold, the angel of the Lord came upon him, and a light shined in the prison: and he smote Peter on the side, and raised him up, saying, Arise up quickly. And his chains fell off from his hands.

In the book of Acts, the ministry of angels was a common occurrence: *"Are they not all ministering spirits, sent forth to minister for them who shall be heirs of salvation? Therefore we ought to give the more earnest heed to the things which we have heard, lest at any time we should let them slip" (Hebrews 1:14, 2:1).*

Note that it didn't say that angels were sent forth to minister *to* them; it said they were sent forth to minister *for* them. When I am out of town, I have somebody else minister for me. The word *slip* in the Greek text means *to let them leak out.*

Acts 12:7-10
And, behold, the angel of the Lord came upon him, and a light shined in the prison: and he smote Peter on the

side, and raised him up, saying, Arise
up quickly. And his chains fell off from
his hands. And the angel said unto him,
Gird thyself, and bind on thy sandals.
And so he did. And he saith unto him,
Cast thy garment about thee, and follow me. And he went out, and followed
him; and wist not that it was true which
was done by the angel; but thought he
saw a vision. When they were past the
first and the second ward, they came
unto the iron gate that leadeth unto the
city; which opened to them of his own
accord: and they went out, and passed
on through one street; and forthwith the
angel departed from him.

Peter was sleeping so hard that angel had to smack
him and pick him up. The ministry of angels was involved in giving some instructions.

Hebrews 13:1-2
Let brotherly love continue. Be not for-
getful to entertain strangers: for thereby
some have entertained angels un-
awares.

We are getting closer and closer to the end times,
and the ministry of angels is going to be revealed more
and more, just as it was in the book of Acts. In Acts

chapter 12, the angel leaves and Peter goes and knocks on the door of the house where people are praying for him. A girl named Rhoda answers the door, and she runs back in crying, *"It's Peter! It's Peter!"*

The whole gathering says, *"No it must be his angel."* This isn't a strange thing to say for people who had many angelic visitations.

Romans 4:18-20
Who against hope believed in hope, that he might become the father of many nations, according to that which was spoken, So shall thy seed be. And being not weak in faith, he considered not his own body now dead, when he was about an hundred years old, neither yet the deadness of Sarah's womb: He staggered not at the promise of God through unbelief; but was strong in faith, giving glory to God.

If Abraham wasn't considering his own body, what was he considering? He was considering the promise of God. Strong faith considers the Word. Weak faith considers the circumstance. When you get a word from God, you do what Abraham did. He was fully persuaded that the Lord was able to perform what the Lord had promised. God liked that so much that it was imputed to him for righteousness. Again, God is talking to you every day about everything in your life. I want to caution you not to run with the crowd. In John chapter six, Jesus said that His flesh was meat indeed and His blood was drink indeed *(verse 55)*, those who ate His flesh and drank His blood would dwell in Him and He in them *(verse 56)*, and that those who are this bread would live forever *(verse 58)*.

> **John 6:60-61**
> Many therefore of his disciples, when they had heard this, said, This is an hard saying; who can hear it? When Jesus knew in himself that his disciples murmured at it, he said unto them, Doth this offend you?

When somebody starts murmuring, you should say, *"Bye-bye. I can't be part of that."*

> **John 6:66-67**
> From that time many of his disciples went back, and walked no more with him. Then said Jesus unto the twelve, Will ye also go away?

Jesus preached a sermon in the synagogue; the people were offended at what He preached, and they said, *"We aren't following you any more."* They were seed by the wayside. When many walked away, did Jesus get upset and say, *"Everybody's leaving me."* No. Jesus said to the twelve, *"Do you want to go too?"*

John 6:68-69
Then Simon Peter answered him, Lord, to whom shall we go? thou hast the words of eternal life. And we believe and are sure that thou art that Christ, the Son of the living God.

The Word tells you that perilous times will come and many will fall away from the faith. Don't follow the crowd. Follow the word from God. No word from God is void of power. Every word has enough power in it to cause you to walk in the impossible. One word from God calls Peter to walk on the water. All you need is one word from God, and one word from God can cause you to win all the time.

Faith can only be activated when the will of God is known. I was a sinner, but I heard a word from God on salvation. And when that word came, I made a decision to believe it. Faith came with it. I did what Romans 10:9-10 told me to do:

Romans 10:9-10
That if thou shalt confess with thy mouth the Lord Jesus, and shalt believe in thine heart that God hath raised him from the dead, thou shalt be saved. For with the heart man believeth unto righteousness; and with the mouth confession is made unto salvation.

God spoke to me through a minister who preached the Word. When I acted upon the Word, a supernatural event changed a heathen to a channel of God, suddenly!

9

Acting, Talking and Living in Faith

Many people read Hebrews chapter 11 when they start studying about faith, but Hebrews 11:1 begins, *"Now faith is . . ."* In other words, this could read, *"Wherefore faith is . . ."* or *"But faith is . . ."* You don't start a discussion with the word now. Obviously, Paul is referencing things that he has been talking about prior to this verse; this is a continuation of verses dealing with that subject. In this chapter, I'm going to look at eight things in Hebrews chapter 10 that build the foundation for living by faith.

In Hebrews chapter 10, Paul talks about the law and how the law didn't have the power to make us clean and holy before God. He goes on to talk about how the law had its limits, and then gives the purpose of the law. If the law could have made man righteous before God, then nothing else would have needed to come after it. Continuing in Hebrews, Paul explains further.

Hebrews 10:10
By the which will we are sanctified
[made holy, set apart] through the offering of the body of Jesus Christ once for
all.

Paul makes the point that the sacrifice of Jesus
was once and for all, because under the law, the priests
offered a daily sacrifice to cover–not eradicate–your sin.
Jesus came and offered Himself once and forever.

Hebrews 10:11-13
And every priest standeth daily ministering and offering oftentimes the same
sacrifices, which can never take away
sins: But this man, after he had offered
one sacrifice for sins for ever, sat down
on the right hand of God; From hence-
forth expecting till his enemies be made
his footstool.

This man, Jesus, sat down expecting that those who
live by faith would place His enemies under His feet.
God's expectation is that we be faith people and live
by faith. **He expects us to dominate the devil; He
doesn't expect the devil to dominate us.**

In the body of Christ, Jesus is the head, and we
are the body, as seen in both *Ephesians 1:23* and *First
Corinthians 12:13*. Jesus said that He's expecting us
to keep His enemies under our feet. That is one of the

reasons why God gave you faith. He didn't give you faith for a Cadillac or for a 10,000 square feet house. There's nothing wrong with those things, unless whatever you possess owns you and becomes gods before the one true God.

No More Sin Consciousness
Hebrews 10:14-17

For by one offering he hath perfected for ever them that are sanctified. Whereof the Holy Ghost also is a witness to us: for after that he had said before, This is the covenant that I will make with them after those days, saith the Lord, I will put my laws into their hearts, and in their minds will I write them; And their sins and iniquities will I remember no more.

To become a strong faith person and walk by faith and not by sight, you must know that you are forgiven, cleansed and in fellowship with God. Jesus was righteous, and we were sinners. We received His righteousness, and He took upon Himself our sins. That was unfair, but I will take the deal! If you don't know that you are in right-standing with God, Satan will find a way to beat you around and place doubt in your heart about whether or not what you are believing for will come to pass. He will tell you that you aren't worthy. If you aren't worthy after Jesus did all that, then His death and resurrection was of no value. God didn't do

Now the just shall live by faith: but if any man draw back, my soul shall have no pleasure in him. But we are not of them who draw back unto perdition; but of them that believe to the saving of the soul.

As we have seen, walking in patience is essential to living by faith. Without patience, you will grow weary and give in to doubt, fear and unbelief. Without patience, you will not reap the harvest God desires to give you. Without patience, you will not have a solid foundation on which to build a life of faith.

10

Hearing Words About Words

Words locate your faith level. Faith-filled words are soothing to the soul, but doubt-filled words destroy it. In this chapter, I am going to give you verses from the book of Proverbs concerning the importance of your words. When God repeats himself twice, He is making a major emphasis. In Proverbs, there are more than forty references to the subject of your words, which means that you need to pay major attention to this subject. **How you use words will determine the degree to which your faith is operative.** God's will is to turn your situation around, because whatever you are dealing with is temporary and is subject to change if it is negative.

You are to *"hold fast the profession of our faith without wavering" (Hebrews 10:23)*, and using your words well enable you to do that. Let's look at some verses that give you insight into what happens if you do that

Proverbs 14:3 tells us that *"in the mouth of the foolish is a rod of pride: but the lips of the wise shall preserve them.* The word *preserve* means *to protect.* **You can protect yourself, your family, your money, and your life with your mouth, setting spiritual forces at work.**

Proverbs 18:21
Death and life are in the power of the tongue: and they that love it shall eat the fruit thereof.

The word *power* in Hebrew refers to *the means and direction of something.* The means of death or the means of life are in the tongue, and you will consume the reward of whatever you say.

Proverbs 16:1
The preparations of the heart in man, and the answer of the tongue, is from the LORD.

The word *answer* means *the reply of the Lord.* God has something to do with the systems of the Lord! God created the Earth and everything within through the power of His words. God said, *"Let us make man in our image, after our likeness. Let's make him do what I do and like I do it."* God said it, and it was so.

You can turn that which was created against you and destroy it, too. If God said, *"You are damned,"* what do you think would happen? God never intended for words to be negatively applied.

When Adam and Eve sinned in the Garden of Eden, the punishments began. After God created Adam, He said, *"Adam, I am going to let all the animals go before you, and they will be whatever you name them."* God had given man the responsibility of taking care of the Garden. Before the curse, Adam took care of the Garden with his words, not with his hands and with sweat. Adam was in the likeness of God; he spoke, and it came to pass. After Adam and Eve sinned, God said, *"No longer will the ground yield the way it used to. The ground will yield thorns and thistles, and you will have to work it with sorrow and sweat all the days of your life."*

Man's words still have that force, negatively and positively. If you were in an auditorium where a person was waving a loaded 12-gauge, you would be diving under a chair because you would know that you could get killed. Likewise, death and life are in the power of the tongue. **Faith-filled words dominate the laws of sin and death.**

Proverbs 10:11
The mouth of a righteous man is a well of life: but violence covereth the mouth of the wicked.

The Hebrew word for *well* is *source*. The source of something is where it comes from; thus, *"The mouth of a righteous man is a source of life."* The mouth of the wicked is the source of death: *"A man shall eat good by the fruit of his mouth: but the soul of the transgressors shall eat violence" (Proverbs 13:2).* The word *fruit* means *reward.* Your words reward you. You get what you deserve based on what you have been saying. All the good stuff in your life is a result of saying faith-filled words.

Proverbs 18:20
A man's belly shall be satisfied with the fruit of his mouth; and with the increase of his lips shall he be filled.

In Hebrew, the word *increase* means *income.* A man's provisions shall be satisfied with the reward of his mouth, and with the income of his lips shall he be filled. Recently, many Christians started saying, *"This is the greatest recession since the Great Depression."* People started losing their jobs and stopped buying goods because they got into fear. They turned the shotgun on themselves. They started saying what the media was saying instead of going to the Word and releasing life and income. Instead of saying what God said, they started saying what the world said, and they got exactly what the world got. They didn't use their force that God had given them for life and for increase.

When you're in a tough spot, go right to the Bible, because you want your situation to change. The definition of *insanity* is *to do the same thing over and over and expect a different result.* If you keep talking like the world, speaking like the world and reacting like the world, why are you surprised that nothing is happening? Don't say, *"Oh I don't understand why God let this happen to me?"* God didn't let it happen. You did. He told you what to do about it. He gave you a force. He gave you a power that will release His ability to work in your life, but you have authority in this Earth and you can decide what happens or what doesn't happen in your life. God gave you free will. He gave you choice, and you can choose to say what He says or you can choose to say what you see. You should walk by faith, not by sight. A great deal of walking by faith requires keeping your mouth in check and speaking only faith-filled words in the midst of contrary situations.

Proverbs 12:14
A man shall be satisfied with good by the fruit of his mouth: and the recompence of a man's hands shall be rendered unto him.

To be *satisfied* means *you have so much good that you don't have room for any more.* It's like when your mother fixes a big meal on the holiday, and you sit there and eat until you can't take one more bite.

"Son, do you want some more?"

"I can't eat one more bite mom! I am satisfied!"

Proverbs 10:21
The lips of the righteous feed many: but fools die for want of wisdom.

take. Satan then tempts you to say, *"All this bad stuff is happening to me."* As a result, you will keep getting lower and lower and lower. If you can turn your mouth around, you will have a chance to move higher: *"A man hath joy by the answer of his mouth: and a word spoken in due season, how good is it" (Proverbs 15:23)!*

That's why Paul and Silas were delivered in Acts chapter 16 after they had been beaten and stripped in the public square and put in prison. At midnight, rather than complain, Paul and Silas began to pray and sing praises, and they had a miracle. God's power created an earthquake and they were loosed from that situation. God's hands would have been tied if they had kept speaking what they saw and what they felt and what had happened. Because they did the opposite, they loosed the power of God because they gave Him permission to turn around their situation.

Proverbs 24:26
Every man shall kiss his lips that giveth a right answer.

You see power working on your behalf when you give the right answer. The right answer is found in God's Word.

Proverbs 14:7
Go from the presence of a foolish man, when thou perceivest not in him the lips of knowledge.

Don't let your ears be a trash can. If you do, don't be surprised if you are contaminated. If somebody is knocking God's truth, get away from that person. You can't afford to be around people like that. All of my friends talk one way—God's way. If somebody starts talking unbelief, we immediately will correct one another. Why? Because it is dangerous to do that.

Proverbs 17:28
Even a fool, when he holdeth his peace, is counted wise: and he that shutteth his lips is esteemed a man of understanding.

Even if you are a fool, nobody will know it if you keep your mouth shut. Instead, people will think you are smart. Believer, you have this unction inside of you that says, *"Shut up. Don't talk."* That is the Holy Ghost, because He wants to be in position to help you with His power. But you can stop the power with your mouth. The parents of John the Baptist, Zechariah and Elisabeth, had been praying all their lives for a child and were now old. An angel showed up while Zechariah was in the temple doing the daily ministrations of a priest and said, *"Rejoice. Your prayers have been heard. You are going to have a son. Call his name John."*

Zechariah said, *"How is that going to happen?"*

The angel said, *"Because you opened your mouth, you will be struck dumb and will not speak until after the child is born."* Why would that be the case? If Zech-

Hebrews 4:14
Seeing then that we have a great high priest, that is passed into the heavens, Jesus the Son of God, let us hold fast our profession.

Jesus is not offering up words such as *"I am full of fear"* or *"We are losing."* He's not taking the statement, *"I don't know what I can do. I am sick, sad and discouraged."* No. Those are not acceptable to the Father because those are not faith-filled words. Those are words of doubt and unbelief.

Thus, our words determine whether we will have a manifestation we desire or one we don't desire. Our words determine whether or not our great High Priest can go before the Father on our behalf or whether He has to sit on the sidelines and watch us being destroyed because we allowed Satan to work against us with our negative words.

There's a great story about Babe Ruth visiting a child that was at the point of death in the hospital. Babe told the child, *"I am going to hit a home run for you in the next game."* The newspapers published Babe's comment, so the other team was alerted. The first time Babe came up to bat, the other team walked him. They walked him the second, third and fourth time, because they knew he was charged up to hit one out of the ballpark. Eventually, the pitcher made a mistake and threw a pitch too close to the plate, and Babe reached over and hit it out. In other words, he called it before it happened.

Faith is calling it before you swing. God wants trust and confidence before you see results.

The Relationship Between Faith and Patience

This trust and confidence is evident when you wait in patience. Patience is a dirty word for many Christians, because we live in the age of immediate gratification. To be *patient* means to *remain constant, steadfast and unmovable.*

In Colossians chapter one, look at what the Apostle Paul prays for the church at Colosse: *"For this cause we also, since the day we heard it, do not cease to pray for you, and to desire that ye might be filled with the knowledge of his will in all wisdom and spiritual understanding. That ye might walk worthy of the Lord unto all pleasing, being fruitful in every good work, and increasing in the knowledge of God; Strengthened with all might, according to his glorious power, unto all patience and longsuffering with joyfulness"* (Colossians 1:9-11).

He said, *"I am praying that patience be part of the mix you bring to receiving supernatural knowledge, a manifestation of the wisdom of God."* Paul preached that to the church of Thessalonica too.

2 Thessalonians 1:2-4

Grace unto you, and peace, from God our Father and the Lord Jesus Christ. We are bound to thank God always for you, brethren, as it is meet, because that your faith groweth exceedingly,

> and the charity of every one of you all
> toward each other aboundeth; So that
> we ourselves glory in you in the churches
> of God for your patience and faith in all
> your persecutions and tribulations that
> ye endure.

In other words, he said, *"Persecutions and tribulations are coming against you, and you have trust, confidence and reliance on God. It doesn't matter how much pressure comes against you—remain the same."* That is patience.

The Lord gave me several truths about patience. *First,* without patience your faith will short circuit. Faith is a force working on the problem the whole time. You may not see anything in the natural, but your faith is out working on that problem. It will work as long as you keep it out there. The moment you stop operating in faith, you stop the work. It's as if a logger were three-quarters of the way through cutting down a tree but decided to quit since he hadn't seen it fall. There was nothing wrong with the axe. There was nothing wrong with his arm. He just quit too soon. If he had kept going, the tree would eventually have fallen.

The *second* thing about patience is that it requires faith in order to achieve a manifestation. Someone may be patient; in fact, he may be constant all the time, but he doesn't expect anything to happen. In reality, he's said to himself, *"I'm done. I'm not fighting any more."* Patience in tribulation, without faith, is giving up. Faith and patience need to work together. Patience without faith is wishful thinking. Many Christians are waiting on God to move, but they have not exercised any faith. When asked what they are doing, they say, *"We're waiting on God."* They aren't waiting on God, however; God is waiting on them.

Faith, once again, is acting on what you believe. But after you have acted, you need patience so that the force that you have sent to work can stay out there and keep working, however long it takes. If a logger is chopping down a little tree, it may take only one or two blows with his axe. But if he is cutting down a California redwood, it will take a whole lot longer to fell that tree.

The small tree and the large tree are symbolic of the size of the problem you may be dealing with. If you have a small problem, a few whacks with your faith will take care of it. However, some of you have been building redwoods. You have dug yourself into massive debt for a decade. You have been poisoning your body for twenty-five years. You have a redwood-sized problem, but you want the thing to fall in your life as if it were a tiny tree.

Every time that axe of faith goes into the tree, every time you say what God said, it is doing something, but it's going to take time. You may say, *"I am just tired of swinging and I don't see anything happening."* If you throw your axe on the ground and walk away, your problem will still be there. You have to have faith until it falls. There are instant manifestations of miracles in the Word of God, but that is not the norm in the Scripture. Why? Because the Biblical principle is that a man reaps what he sows. You may have *"to cast thy bread upon the waters and find it after many days" (Ecclesiastes 11:1)*. What do you do between the time you cast your bread on the water and the time it comes back? You wait patiently. You endure, giving God praise and glory.

1 Timothy 6:11-12
But thou, O man of God, flee these things; and follow after righteousness, godliness, faith, love, patience, meekness. Fight the good fight of faith, lay hold on eternal life, whereunto thou art also called, and hast professed a good profession before many witnesses.

2 Peter 3:8-9
But, beloved, be not ignorant of this one thing, that one day is with the Lord as a thousand years, and a thousand years as one day. The Lord is not slack concerning his promise, as some men count slackness; but is longsuffering to us-ward, not willing that any should perish, but that all should come to repentance.

The context of these verses is a discussion about the second coming of the Lord, but there is a principle in it that is very true. Namely, that God does not see time the same way that we do. In other words, with us, thirty years is a long time, but with God, thirty years is nothing. God doesn't see things based on a clock.

I know this to be a fact, and I am going to talk experientially. I have been in the ministry for more than thirty-six years, and I can tell you that everything the Lord has ever told me has come to pass except a few things that I am still waiting for patiently. The Lord said many things to me that I thought were right around the corner, but they didn't come in my time frame.

Many Christians get a prophecy, a Word from the Lord, and think, *"It's going to happen."* When it doesn't happen next week and when it doesn't happen the week after, they think, *"Maybe I didn't hear from God."* The problem isn't that they didn't hear from God, but that God is not operating on their timetable.

There are things the Lord has said to me, and I knew without any doubt that they were from God. One time, it took thirteen years before what God said came to pass. It happened exactly as God had told me. For thirteen years, I had to exercise faith and patience. There are things that I've forgotten, but God never forgets one promise.

God doesn't operate based on our time, and I will give you my opinion on the matter from having walked with Him for this period of time. I believe there are two reasons why things take so long. *One reason* is because they aren't supposed to come to pass until later. God has foreknowledge, and He is setting things up. The *second reason* I believe things get delayed is because we delay them. We mess up. We get off course.

God said that Elisha would replace Elijah, but it was twenty years before that came to pass. During that twenty years, Elisha had to serve Elijah. People knew he was called, but it wasn't time; Elisha didn't get out of sorts about it.

You might have a calling to be a prophet, but that doesn't mean you are supposed to stand in that office right now. The reason many people are messed up is because God speaks to them and gives them some calling, and off they run without knowing what they are doing. They aren't trained. They don't have patience. Their ministry goes nowhere. Elisha had to be faithful for twenty years. **Patience and faith work together.**

Living by faith requires development of patience, this force of the spirit. All four Gospels give us the parable of the sower and the Word of God and how the Word will produce thirty-fold, sixty-fold and one hundred fold. Jesus told us how Satan short circuits the Word by using five tools: *affliction, persecution, cares of this world, deceitfulness of riches,* and *lust of other things.* These things enter in and choke the Word, and it becomes unfruitful. But Jesus also tells us that the individual who is on good ground and has the Word in him doesn't fall for Satan's strategies, and because of that, the Word will produce ten thousand percent.

Let's look at this parable in Luke chapter eight: *"Now the parable is this: The seed is the word of God.*

Those by the way side are they that hear; then cometh the devil, and taketh away the word out of their hearts, lest they should believe and be saved.

They on the rock are they, which, when they hear, receive the word with joy; and these have no root, which for a while believe, and in time of temptation fall away.

And that which fell among thorns are they, which, when they have heard, go forth, and are choked with cares and riches and pleasures of this life, and bring no fruit to perfection.

But that on the good ground are they, which in an honest and good heart, having heard the word, keep it, and bring forth fruit with patience" (Luke 8:11-15).

They heard the Word and then acted on what they heard. Then they were patient. They remained constant and steadfast through afflictions, persecutions, cares of this world, deceitfulness of riches and lust of other things. They didn't change, no matter what Satan threw at them. They stayed on the Word. They believed the Word. They acted on the Word, and they brought forth the will of God.

The will of God is not automatic. See some people think that whatever God wants to happen will happen, and there's nothing they can do about it. It is God's will that all men be saved and come into the knowledge of the truth (*see 1 Timothy 2:2*), but the same Bible tells you that many will go to Hell. If God wants everyone to be saved, how come some will not be? Because people make that choice.

So even though it is God's will for you to be healed, for your bills to be paid, for you to be safe and for your children to follow God, people are free moral agents on this Earth. Your words matter. Your actions matter. As a man sows, he reaps. God tells you what to do to see His will comes to pass, but if you give up on Him, give up on His Word and give up on your faith, you'll be by the wayside and won't bring forth. In order to bring forth, in order to inherit the promises (*Hebrews 6:12*), you need both faith and patience.

The Importance of Eager Expectations

One of the reasons why people don't walk in patience is that they are too lazy to do spiritual work. They are too lazy to daily give thanksgiving to God, pray in the Spirit, meditate the Word, confess the Word over themselves, decide to walk in love, be open to the Holy Spirit and give. Because they are lazy, they do not have enough power to be patient. Then they don't inherit the promise, and they say, *"I don't know why God let this happen to me."* It wasn't God's fault. They were the problem.

The good news is that if you are the problem, you can turn around and be the answer. Hebrews chapter six talks about a man named Abraham who didn't start out walking in faith and patience but learned to operate that way. As a result, he was blessed in all things.

You have to know who you are in Christ, you have to live holy, you have to clean up your mouth, you have to realize that you have a High Priest, you have to keep your body in line, and you have to keep your confession and remain constant, even in the middle of the storm in your life.

Hebrews 10:35
Cast not away therefore your confidence, which hath great recompence of reward.

The word *confidence* means *boldness of speech.* When you're in a tough situation, don't stop speaking words of faith. Speak to the mountain. Jesus Himself, the King of kings and the Lord of lords, is in the middle of your tough situation offering up your faith words to the Father. He is saying, *"Father, this child of yours has confidence and trust in you. My blood caused him to be cleansed. Father, you said that you were pleased when he does that, so we are expecting manifestation in his behalf."* And that is exactly what you are going to get!

Hebrews 10:36-39
For ye have need of patience, that, after ye have done the will of God, ye might receive the promise. For yet a little while, and he that shall come will come, and will not tarry.

Now the just shall live by faith: but if any man draw back, my soul shall have no pleasure in him.

> But we are not of them who draw back
> unto perdition; but of them that believe
> to the saving of the soul.

You have to understand this race with God. You are either in or you are out. You have to make a decision about this. The closer you get to the end and the coming of our Lord, the more you'll find that the middle ground has all been burned out. You are not going to be able to hide. You are not going to be able to have one foot in the world and one foot in God, too.

The person who doesn't please God is the one that draws back. When you set your faith on something, you have to make a decision that you are setting your faith there until you die. Drawing back only results in the defeat and entrapment. You have to decide that you're not going back to debt, sickness, fear, anger and strife. Choose life! Choose healing and debt-free living. Choose joy and love!

12

Dealing With Pressure

I n all areas of life, you want to be successful and experience victory, but many times you don't know what you need to do in order to live as an overcomer. What do you do when you're trying to walk in faith and patience and the pressure is on? How do you respond when you hit obstacles again and again? Let's look at several passages in the Word of God that give direction and encouragement.

Hebrews 12:1a

Wherefore seeing we also are com-
passed about with so great a cloud of
witnesses, let us lay aside every weight,
and the sin which doth so easily beset
us.

The great a cloud of witnesses is comprised of all those people who received victory by faith. They are our role models. In order to get where they are, we need to lay aside the things or weights that get in our way.

No doubt there will be people who get in your way. They may drag you to sin and drag you away from God. You may say, *"Oh, they need me."* As a believer, it is your responsibility to share the Word of God with them, but at that point you have to let them decide which way they want to go. They have a choice to make, just as you do. As a pastor, I have learned that all I can do is put the Word out there and let people make their own decisions. I have to live with the choices they make.

People have free will, and if they want to go to Hell or if they want to have less than what God has provided for them, that is their decision. You have to do what you have to do because you are going to stand before God, too. However, you're only going to be responsible for the choices you made, not for the choices others made.

That's even true relative to your children. When your children get to a certain age, they are grown human beings. You don't treat grown people like children. You allow them to decide to do what they are going to do, and then you let them live with the consequences. When they start living with the consequences of their actions, they will come to understand quickly why you had been saying what you said. My only son chose to follow God, but if he had wound up in jail at eighteen or nineteen, I would not have tried to rescue him.

You may say, *"Don't you love him?"* You better believe I love my son. But if he had decided to go contrary to the way of God, that would have been his decision. It wouldn't have been because I was a bad parent, because from the time he came into this world, I taught him the Word. If he had made poor decisions, I would have let him reap the consequences, and when he got out of jail, I think he would have been listening! Thank God, my son chose to follow God. He is a preacher of the Gospel and has a beautiful family that loves God. He received the Word and acted on it because he chose to do so.

Hebrews 12:1b
And let us run with patience **[endurance]** the race that is set before us.

You are in a race that you have to run with consistency. You value consistency. For example, when you get in your car and turn the key, you want it to start every time. If you want it to work every time, you have to do some things to keep it working: change the sparks and plugs, change the oil and keep that battery powered.

You are involved in a life race. God has given you a huge battery, and it is called faith. It will power you wherever you want to go. When your battery is kept charged, even though you might be in situation where things don't look too good, you can run through rain, you can drive through wind and you can go through all kinds of stuff. You may not see much light right now, but if you stay on the road, you are going to hit some sunshine. If you drive long enough, you are going to find some daylight.

Hebrews 12:2
Looking unto Jesus the author and
finisher of our faith; who for the joy that
was set before him endured the cross,
despising the shame, and is set down at
the right hand of the throne of God.

Jesus began our journey of faith, and He's the One
who develops our faith. In ministry, as in every area of
life, there are people who want to have success, but they
don't want to do what they need to do to be successful. A
man reaps what he sows; Scripture does not say that a
man sows and another man reaps. It is not scriptural at
all for me to plant and someone else to harvest. It's not
God's way.

In fact, to want something that somebody else
worked for is covetousness, and Scripture says, *"Thou
shalt not covet."* If you are forcing someone to give to
you, then you are stealing the fruit of his labor. There
are people who want to reap a big harvest, but they
don't want to consistently sow the seed.

Hebrews 12:3
For consider him that endured such con-
tradiction of sinners against himself, lest
ye be wearied and faint in your minds
[or emotions and will].

In other words, consider Jesus; consider what God
said. If you don't know what God said or you are too lazy

to find out what He said, you won't have anything to consider. And that's how you lose.

Keep Your Soul in Patience

Jesus is prophesying about tough times ahead for these Jewish believers, and He said, *"In your patience possess ye your souls" (Luke 21:19).* A time is coming when they are going to be under great persecution, and He says, *"In your patience–in consistency and cheerful endurance–do not lose your mind, will and emotions."* Making a decision to walk in patience keeps you grounded in the middle of trouble. Patience is what you need when something seems to have you around the throat.

It's just like when you plant a seed in the ground and cover it up with dirt. You water it and don't see something come up the next day. In fact, it may be weeks, months or even a year before you see any evidence that anything is happening. The seed didn't start growing when the blade popped up through the dirt, however. It was growing all the time when you couldn't see it.

Too many Christians give up too quickly. They say, *"Oh woe is me. I really do feel bad, and I am just going to lay here."* No! Drag your body out of bed and join with other believers. Laying in bed isn't going to get you healed. If you can't get out of the bed, then roll out on the floor. You have to fight the good fight of faith, and the good fight of faith requires faith and patience.

In the Revelation of Jesus Christ given by an angel to John, he writes to seven churches in Asia Minor. For each church, John identifies things that Jesus likes in the churches and the things that He doesn't like.

Revelation 2:1-3
Unto the angel of the church of Ephesus write; These things saith he that holdeth the seven stars in his right hand, who walketh in the midst of the seven golden candlesticks; I know thy works, and thy labour, and thy patience, and how thou canst not bear them which are evil: and thou hast tried them which say they are apostles, and are not, and hast found them liars: And hast borne, and hast patience, and for my name's sake hast laboured, and hast not fainted.

One of the things about which Jesus commends the church is their patience. In other words, He says, *"You have cheerful endurance any time the enemy comes against you."* Would He commend you if He looked at you? Look at His words to the church at Thyatira:

Revelation 2:18-19
And unto the angel of the church in Thyatira write; These things saith the Son of God, who hath his eyes like unto a flame of fire, and his feet are like fine brass; I know thy works, and charity, and service, and faith, and thy patience,

and thy works; and the last to be more
than the first.

He commends them for faith; He commends them
for love; He commends them for patient endurance.
God is pleased when you say, *"I believe God, and I don't
change my words. I don't change my actions. I have a
cheerful attitude. I win. I may not see any thing different
right now, but I'm standing in faith and patience for as
long as it takes."*

Titus 2:1-2
But speak thou the things which become sound doctrine: That the aged
[mature] men be sober **[vigilant]**, grave,
temperate, sound in faith, in charity, in
patience.

Patience is the hallmark of maturity. Lack of patience is the hallmark of immaturity, both naturally and
spiritually. An immature man or immature woman has
to do everything right now.

That characterizes many young people. They do
everything fast because they are immature. They don't
know yet that they need to wait.

Young men, I know that woman is fine, but wait.
Everything that glitters isn't gold. She can have a
beautiful body, but she can be rotten inside. Young man,
don't buy a car just because it looks nice. You need to do
your homework. You need to find out how many miles

really are on the tires. You need to find out how many revolutions are on this fan belt.

Maturity not only has faith, but also can walk in love. In other words, a mature person doesn't get into strife, which can short circuit faith. Once you believe God and say it with your mouth, you can walk in patience, however long it takes.

There are instant manifestations of things in the Word, but we look not at things which are seen but at things that are not seen. The things which are seen are temporary, which means subject to change *(2 Corinthians 4:18)*. If the Word is telling you not to look at what you see, then that must mean that everything is not instant. Let's take a look at what to do when the pressure is on.

Get in the Word Every Day
Romans 15:4
> For whatsoever things were written
> aforetime were written for our learning,
> that we through patience and comfort
> of the scriptures might have hope.

My wife desires to be with her grandchildren, who live an hour away, and the Word says that the Lord gives you the desires of your heart. We recently decided to sell the house we bought three years ago and move closer to family. The realtor warned us about the bad market conditions when we put it up for sale. The Word says that when you sow, you shall reap. My wife and I

Dealing with Pressure

sow huge seed. We are givers, and we give every day. We have a harvest coming. Since we know that we have comfort and hope through the Scriptures, we are not looking at the newspaper every day with all the bad housing reports. My hope is not dead. I am not saying, *"I was hoping the market would be getting better; instead it's getting worse."* Why? Every day I take a dose of hope, a dose of comfort and a dose of faith. And that causes me to be patient.

Have a Victory Attitude
James 1:1-2

James, a servant of God and of the Lord Jesus Christ, to the twelve tribes which are scattered abroad, greeting. My brethren, count it all joy when ye fall into divers temptations.

The word *temptations* means *test, trials, problems and pressures.* These people–because of their disobedience–have been run out of their homes and out of their countries. They have been dispersed.

Believers face pressure, but this Scripture says to count it all joy. The word joy means to come to life. To count something joy means you have a decision to make. You can say, *"Oh, what's happening? I am so upset."* Or you can say, *"I want to thank you, Lord. I give you praise and glory. This situation is going down, too."*

This is not a natural response unless you become a Word person. All your life, you've been taught that when things go bad you drop your head, utter negative things, and let your shoulders droop. That all affects your attitude. You can't count it all joy in your natural man. That only becomes your normal response–and it can become normal–if every day you renew your mind. When a bad deal comes to you say, *"Thank you, Father. That is another opportunity for victory."*

James 1:3
Knowing this, that the trying of your faith worketh patience.

The person with the right attitude and right mouth, the person that keeps the joyful attitude, the person whose mind is renewed by the Word of God, has an attitude that says, *"This test and trial isn't going to wipe me out. This tribulation is going to make me more patient. God's power in this test is going to make me stronger."*

James 1:4
But let patience have her perfect work, that ye may be perfect and entire, wanting nothing.

Stay constant on the Word of God. Say what God's Word said. Sow good seed. Walk in love. If you stand on the Word of God, your faith force is working on that tribulation. Is it a test and trial? Yes, but you can count it as joy. Why? Because the axe is cutting into that tribulation. Every time you say, *"God supplies my needs.*

He has made a way for me. The peace of God works on my behalf. The angels of God are with me. No weapon is going against me," your faith is working on that tree. In God's time, that tree will fall. And the next time another tree is in the middle of your life, you will say, *"God brought me out the last time, and he will do it this time."*

Romans 5:1-5
Therefore being justified by faith, we have peace with God through our Lord Jesus Christ: By whom also we have access by faith into this grace wherein we stand, and rejoice in hope of the glory of God.

And not only so, but we glory in tribulations also: knowing that tribulation worketh patience; And patience, experience; and experience, hope: And hope maketh not ashamed; because the love of God is shed abroad in our hearts by the Holy Ghost which is given unto us.

The word *tribulation* is *pressure*. You rejoice in the face of pressure. You rejoice in the face of tests and trials. You rejoice when the problem seems too big. You keep your faith working on that mountain. You go to church as much as you can, because it will remind you to rejoice. But when you are not at church, when you get up in the morning and you don't feel well, you rejoice. When the bill is still there, you rejoice. When someone is talking about you, rejoice.

Patience helps bring the experience of victory and the experience of hope. You experience God bringing you through a trial, and the next time you say, *"He did it last time, and He will do it this time."* You have hope, regardless of what the situation is. It may take you a while to get out of it, but stay with it. Keep that good attitude. Your attitude will determine your altitude.

Ask for Wisdom
James 1:5

If any of you lack wisdom, let him ask of God, that giveth to all men liberally, and upbraideth not; and it shall be given him.

Note that the *"if"* is after the trials, the tests, the pressure and the patience. The context, therefore, is being in the middle of tribulation. The word *wisdom* means *insight into the true nature of things*–what's going on, how it is working, and where the attack is coming from.

The God who gives wisdom giveth liberally. He will give you wisdom about how you got in the problem, what door you opened, and how to shut it and fix it. As soon as you know what to do, unless you like pain, you are going to do something about it. But note the next few verses: *"But let him ask in faith, nothing wavering.*

For he that wavereth is like a wave of the sea driven with the wind and tossed. For let not that man think that he shall receive any thing of the Lord. A double minded man is unstable in all his ways" (James 1:6-8).

Don't go to God begging. A man of two minds is unstable. Either stay with God or don't. Either do the Word or know that you are just playing church. You have to make up your mind.

I ask God for wisdom all the time. I say, *"Lord, my head doesn't know what to do, but inside me is the wisdom of God, and the Bible is the wisdom of God, so I am asking you now to show me what I need to know."*

Sometimes the Lord will give you instruction. Sometimes He will give you a word. Sometimes He will give you that bit of adjustment and insight that shows you what to do. God knows everything, including the future, and He will share that if you ask.

Rejoice that Wisdom is Yours
Romans 12:12
Rejoicing in hope; patient in tribulation; continuing instant in prayer.

You remember how God brought a miracle when the enemy attacked Paul and Silas (*Acts 16*). They remained in faith and patience during this attack, rejoicing and praising God. As a result, a miracle came. But when the miracle came, they didn't think that was a sign for them to get out of there. No. Satan has to pay a price for messing with them. Paul and Silas weren't leaving town until they did what God sent them to do. They weren't thinking, *"The doors opened, and we better escape before they come and get us and put us back in the stocks."* No. They were trusting God. The jailer and his entire household were saved, and they established a church there that helped other churches get started.

Understand this. **When the pressure seems to be relieved, don't just go back to what you were doing before.** Instead, say, *"You mess with me devil. Let me see how I can make you feel some pain. Let me snatch somebody from the jaws of Hell that you have been working on for the last thirty years. You've been trying to kill someone prematurely; let me lay hands on that person and see their healing. You've been trying to destroy the union of the people of God with strife; let me walk in love and bring peace to the situation."*

In other words, your attitude has to be, *"I am a victor. I am an overcomer. The Lord is on my side. Faith is on the inside of me. The Holy Ghost is on the inside of me. I have the Word of God, and the Lord's angels are with me. I am not defeated, and I will never be defeated. I will not quit. Greater is He that is in me than that is in the world."*

You may have a setback happen, but just keep on walking, because you know that all the time you are saying what God says, and that tribulation is being chopped down. The bigger the tree, the harder it will fall and the more glory that will come your way. The more opportunities you will have to say, *"See what Jesus has done for me!"*

13

Adding to Your Faith

Wherever faith is present, the Word is present. And wherever the Word is present, faith is present. Thus, when you read, *"Now faith is the substance of things hoped for, the evidence of things not seen" (Hebrews 11:1)*, you can read this verse this way: *"Now the Word of God is the substance of things hoped for."* The Word of God is the evidence, or the confidence, of things that are hoped for. It is the proof of things not seen. When someone asks, *"What is your evidence for this?"* You can say, *"It is written."*

Hebrews 11:2-3
For by it the elders obtained a good report. Through faith we understand that the worlds were framed by the word of God, so that things which are seen were not made of things which do appear.

As we have seen, Abraham had a Word from God, and that is how he obtained a good report.

God reshaped the world by the words of His mouth so that things which are seen were not made of things which do appear. God used His faith and what He said to release His power to change things to what He wanted. If you continue reading Hebrews chapter 11, you'll find many men and women who lived by faith. We live the same way, and we release God's power by the words we say.

2 Peter 1:1

Simon Peter, a servant and an apostle of Jesus Christ, to them that have obtained like precious faith with us through the righteousness of God and our Saviour Jesus Christ.

We received our faith through the death, burial and resurrection of the Lord Jesus Christ and our willingness to accept that. Thus, Peter is talking to us. He then says, *"Grace and peace be multiplied unto you through the knowledge of God, and of Jesus our Lord"* (2 Peter 1:2).

The New Testament is translated from the Greek, and the Greek word for *grace* means *favor, joy, pleasure and liberality. Grace is God's willingness to utilize His power on your behalf; grace is favor.* Some people want to mention the fact that it was unmerited, and it was unmerited. But the Lord Jesus has made you someone that merits it, not because of what you have done, but because of what He has done for you. The grace of God is a manifestation of God.

Peter also pronounces peace. The peace of God surpasses our ability to understand it. The word *peace* means *prosperity, quietness,* and *rest,* and the Greek word for *knowledge* means *full, complete knowledge.* Thus, Peter says, *"Favor, joy, pleasure, liberality, prosperity, quietness and rest abounds unto you through the full, complete knowledge of the Father and the Son."*

2 Peter 1:3
According as his divine power hath given unto us all things that pertain unto life and godliness [holiness], through the knowledge of him that hath called us to glory and virtue.

Supernatural power has been given to you for all things that you deal with–love, relationships, health, children, finances–everything. The more you know, understand and have revealed unto you what God has done for you through the death, burial and resurrection of the Lord Jesus Christ, the more prosperous you will become, the more rest you will receive, the more joy you will experience, and the more freedom you will have. The Word says, *"My people are destroyed for the lack of knowledge"* (*Hosea 4:6a*). Many Christians still think they are supposed to be broke, sick, bad, mad, sad and discouraged, and they think that God is the reason why they are that way; they think that God's their enemy instead of the solution.

2 Peter 1:4
Whereby are given unto us exceeding great and precious [costly] promises: that by these ye might be partakers of the divine nature, having escaped the corruption that is in the world through lust.

The promises are costly because the price paid for them was none other than the shedding of the blood of Jesus. You have the nature of God, and you are a new creature in Christ Jesus *(2 Corinthians 5:17)*. The Holy Spirit of God Himself is located inside of you. You have all His promises, and you have His divine nature. What has that divine nature given you?

You escaped! You are not caught by financial ruin, emotional ruin, physical ruin, family ruin and any other kind of corruption that is in the world system because of this inordinate strong desire, this lust, for other things.

2 Peter 1:5-7
And beside this, giving all diligence, add to your faith virtue; and to virtue knowledge;

And to knowledge temperance; and to temperance patience; and to patience godliness; And to godliness brotherly kindness; and to brotherly kindness charity.

Peter says, *"In addition to all that has been given you, give all diligence."* The word *diligence* is the key to Scriptures everywhere, especially Proverbs. **A diligent person is somebody that keeps on fighting regardless of the opposition.** A diligent person is somebody that puts forth maximum effort. A diligent person is somebody that will do what is required and will not stop.

The next phrase is the heart of this chapter: add to your faith–followed by a list of seven things. Before I start going through these things, notice what happens if you do this.

2 Peter 1:8-10
For if these things be in you, and abound, they make you that ye shall neither be barren nor unfruitful in the knowledge of our Lord Jesus Christ.

But he that lacketh these things is blind, and cannot see afar off **[he has no long range vision]**, and hath forgotten that he was purged from his old sins.

Wherefore the rather, brethren, give diligence to make your calling and

election sure: for if ye do these things, ye
shall never fall.

If you add these seven things to your faith, you will
never fail. Wait a minute! Did Peter say it is possible
for you to never fail? Yes, he did. You just read it in the
Bible. The word *never* means *not at any time*. If you diligently obey this Scripture, you will never, ever lose.

I'm thunderstruck every time I read this passage.
What an amazing promise! Let's find out what those
seven things are and how they work.

Number 1: Add to your faith virtue

The word *virtue* means *valor and excellence*. In other
words, faith requires courage, and it requires doing everything the right way. When you read Hebrews chapter
11, you realize that it took courage for Noah to build
that ark; it took courage for Moses to go before Pharaoh.

A faith man or a faith woman does not operate in
fear. They act with excellence; they don't do anything
halfway. Whatever they do, they do it the right way.

That's why I won't let things be done in certain
ways in the churches I pastor. I could have a lot more
members if I would allow people to start whatever they
want to start and do whatever they want to do, without
drawing the line. But the Word of God tells me that's
not what I am supposed to do.

I am supposed to do everything with excellence, so
we are going to start on time. We are going to do everything with the highest quality that we can, or we aren't

going to do it. That means we have rules and regulations in the church.

Two: And to virtue knowledge

This word *knowledge* means *investigation*. Add to your faith a hunger to find out more, to go deeper in the Word, the way, and the methods of God. I am an investigative reporter. I am not going to stop with this. I am going to keep on burrowing until I find out more truth. God said, *"And ye shall seek me, and find me, when ye shall search for me with all your heart" (Jeremiah 29:13)*. Jesus rose up early, a great while before day, to seek His Father. Many people are not interested in getting up early to seek God.

Three: And to knowledge temperance

The word *temperance* means *self-control*, not God-control. You may say, *"The devil made me do it."* No, he didn't make you do it. He may have waved the temptation in front of your face and said, *"Hey, don't you want that? Look how good that looks."* He may have tempted you, but he can't make you do anything, and God will not make you do anything.

Controlling yourself requires wisdom. It means staying out of some situations and staying away from some folk. It's like somebody who used to have a drinking problem and now feels that God told him to go witness in bars. No, He didn't. Satan has been talking to you. Satan's sending you into that bar, because as soon as you go back in that environment and smell the aroma of that alcohol, as soon as you start thinking about all that stuff you did before, you have taken big steps toward losing self-control. If you are having trouble with an issue, you are to *"Lay aside every weight and the sin which doth so easily beset you" (Hebrews 12:1).* Weight is not a sin. Weight is something that holds you down.

Whatever easily besets you, I have one word for you: **Stay far away from it. Get away.** *"I am strong and I have will power,"* you may say. Don't play the fool. Don't even go there.

Four: And to temperance patience

Add cheerful endurance and consistency. Regardless of what you're facing or how you feel, make a decision to stay true to God's way. Everybody else may be saying something different, but you say what God says.

Five: And to patience godliness

The word *godliness* means *holiness.* Some people think holiness is a denomination–I grew up in a group like that. Holiness is not a denomination. ***Holiness is living as close as possible to what the Scripture says on any subject.*** Women, holiness is not determined by whether or not you wear make-up, a long dress, or have your hair covered. That is religion. God didn't create denominations or religions; men did.

You can have your hair tied up, head covered, wear a long dress, and speak in tongues all day long and be as mean as can be. If that's the case, you are unholy. You are called to live in love. Jesus said, *"If ye love me, keep my commandments" (John 14:15).* He went on the say, *"And he that loveth me shall be loved of my Father, and I will love him, and will manifest myself to him" (John 14:21).* When God is manifested at your point of need, you don't have need any more!

Six: And to godliness brotherly kindness

The words for brotherly kindness in the Greek mean affectionate love of the brethren. He is specifically referring to the fact that your brother is the one who has the same Lord as you do. The Word says, *"As we have therefore opportunity, let us do good unto all men, especially unto them who are of the household of faith" (Galatians 6:10).* We are supposed to have affection for, look out for and help other Christians because they are God's children. Other people are God's creation, but they are not His children. Any parent can tell you that you hate to see your own children in a fight with each other. I used to fight with my brother, and my daddy would break up the fight and say, *"That's your brother."* I would be thinking, *"Yea right, and I am going kill him."* In other words, my father was telling me that blood is thicker than water, and the blood that is thicker than anything else is the blood of Jesus. We are to look past our own well-being to the well-being of others in the family of God.

Seven: And to brotherly kindness charity

Charity is *agapé love.* The objects of brotherly kindness are those in the household of God, and the objects of charity are all of God's creatures. You are to walk with the God-kind of love. God's love sees every person as valuable and precious.

Wherever they are, whatever their situation is, and wherever they come from, you are to walk in love towards them. Galatians 5:6 says that *"Faith worketh (is made active and efficient) by love."*

2 Peter 1:8
For if these things be in you, and abound, they make you that ye shall neither be barren nor unfruitful in the knowledge of our Lord Jesus Christ.

These seven things release God's power in your life, making you fruitful in the knowledge of Jesus. The grace of God—the favor, liberality, and prosperity of God—and the peace of God are both released when you add these seven things to your faith. You propel that power working in your life, and when it's working you can say, *"Good things are happening unto me. God is good to me."*

The reason God is so good to you is that you allowed Him to be good. You released His power by adding these things to your faith. He's ready to bless you, but you need to allow Him to do so.

2 Peter 1:9
But he that lacketh these things is blind, and cannot see afar off, and hath for-

gotten that he was purged from his old
sins.

A blind person is at a disadvantage. A blind person
can't see where he is going. He can't see afar off, which
means he has no long-range vision. The job of the Holy
Ghost is to show you things to come, and without these
seven things, you shut down that ministry. You prohibit
the Holy Spirit from being able to fully show you the future, and without that vision, you will forget what God
rescued you from. You will start acting like a sinner,
even though you have faith. In time you will go back to
your old way, even though you know who God is.

Remember that the devil believes, which means
that faith alone is not enough. Now, faith is vitally important to please God, but alone it is not enough.

2 Peter 1:10
Wherefore the rather, brethren, give
diligence to make your calling and
election sure: for if ye do these things, ye
shall never fall.

You are to make your calling by God sure. You are
to do whatever you need to do. You cement your calling
by adding these seven things to your faith.

If you fall—or fail—it is because you stop operating in these seven things. Stop blaming the devil. Stop
blaming God. Stop trying to rationalize your situation.
Be honest enough to repent and change your behavior.

Failing is not in God's hands; it's in yours. You have to be diligent.

> **2 Peter 1:11**
> For so an entrance shall be ministered unto you abundantly into the everlasting kingdom of our Lord and Saviour Jesus Christ.

The door to the kingdom of God and all the things in it open unto you when you operate in these seven virtues.

> **2 Peter 1:12**
> Wherefore I will not be negligent to put you always in remembrance of these things, though ye know them, and be established in the present truth.

In other words, he's saying, *"I know that you know this, but I am telling you again."* Just because you've heard something doesn't mean that you got it or that you are walking in that truth now. You need to be cautious lest you allow something to slip (*Hebrews 2:1*). The word *slip* in the Greek means *to let it leak out.*

Not too long ago, I was following a truck that was leaking fluid. I doubt that the owner was even aware of that, but one day the red light on his dashboard is going to come on or his engine will have problems because of that leak. That is the way it is with most Christians.

They are leaking, leaking, leaking, but they won't take notice until something happens. Because you heard something doesn't mean you are walking in obedience, and it doesn't mean that you don't need to hear it again.

2 Peter 1:13
Yea, I think it meet, as long as I am in this tabernacle, to stir you up by putting you in remembrance.

Peter was reminding them that they never have to stumble and they never have to fail. Regardless of what you are facing right now or whatever the devil brings down in the future, it won't matter. You are a winner. You are a victor. You are an overcomer. Satan has no power over you.

2 Peter 1:14-15
Knowing that shortly I must put off this my tabernacle, even as our Lord Jesus Christ hath shewed me. Moreover I will endeavour that ye may be able after my decease to have these things always in remembrance.

You should always keep these truths before your eyes. You don't want to forget these things.

2 Peter 1:16-17

For we have not followed cunningly devised fables, when we made known unto you the power and coming of our Lord Jesus Christ, but were eyewitnesses of his majesty. For he received from God the Father honour and glory, when there came such a voice to him from the excellent glory, This is my beloved Son, in whom I am well pleased.

Peter says, *"I didn't just hear about this; I was there. I heard that voice."*

2 Peter 1:18-19

And this voice which came from heaven we heard, when we were with him in the holy mount. We have also a more sure word of prophecy; whereunto ye do well that ye take heed, as unto a light that shineth in a dark place, until the day dawn, and the day star arise in your hearts.

He continues, *"This is more sure and more real than what I saw with my eyes and heard with my ears. It will be well with you if you pay attention to what you do."* Believer, it may be night outside, but do these things until your darkness turns to light. When the sun gets to high noon, there is no darkness anywhere. This is the power of the Word of God, the power of the faith of God, and the power of the things you add to your faith. Satan is afraid of you. Satan can't win. He knows that if you do what you are supposed to do, he can only run.

> **2 Peter 1:20-21**
> Knowing this first, that no prophecy of the scripture is of any private interpretation. For the prophecy came not in old time by the will of man: but holy men of God spake as they were moved by the Holy Ghost.

In other words, this prophecy is available to you whether you are an apostle, a prophet, an evangelist, a teacher or someone whose name is not known. The Holy Ghost is the one who gave you faith.

How do you add these seven things to your faith? *First*, make a decision to do it. Say, *"I am going to be diligent about adding these things to my faith."*

Second, make sure you seek God's wisdom for implementation. *"Lord, show me what I can do to add temperance and more self-control."* He will give you wisdom; the Spirit of God will show you which way to go. The Spirit will say, *"Stop going in that bar"* or *"Satan is using your friend against you. Get away from that person."* He will say, *"You shouldn't go into this debt."* The Holy Ghost will personalize His message to your need.

Third, make sure that you daily do the following:
- Give thanksgiving
- Remain in the Holy Ghost
- Meditate on the Word
- Confess the Word over yourself
- Walk in love
- Stay open to the Holy Spirit
- Be a giver

If you do these things, you will increase in the knowledge of God and of Jesus our Lord. That revelation knowledge will cause you to become more diligent in adding to your faith, which is why Jesus said in Mark chapter four that the rich get richer and the poor get poorer. The man that has will get more because of his diligence, and the man who has not will lose even that which he has because he is not diligent.

Through knowledge of God's Word, you have enough to live by faith, to win by faith and to overcome by faith so that when you get to Heaven your name will be under those listed in the Hall of Faith in Hebrews chapter 11. God will say, *"By faith, you did these things for me. By faith, you overcame through the blood of the Lamb."*

Prayer of Salvation

Heavenly Father, I come to you in the name of Jesus. Your Word says, *"Whosoever shall call on the name of the Lord shall be saved"* and *"If thou shalt confess with thy mouth the Lord Jesus, and shalt believe in thine heart that God hath raised him from the dead, thou shalt be saved"* (*Acts 2:21; Romans 10:9*). You said salvation would be the result of Your Holy Spirit giving me new birth by coming to live in me. I take you at Your Word. Lord Jesus, come into my heart now and be the Lord of my life. I believe that you died for me at Calvary, that you rose from the dead, and are alive forevermore. I receive you as my personal Lord and Savior. Thank you Lord for saving me. I am now born-again.

If you just prayed this prayer, please contact us and let us know. We have a free booklet, *Where Do I Go From Here*, that we would like to send to you. Please call us at 888-909-9673 or visit wordoffaith.cc/faith4lifefreegift.

If you would like to pray with us further, please call 800-541-PRAY (7729). We love you and are here for you.

About the Author

Bishop Keith Butler is the Senior Pastor of faith4life churches in Round Rock and Dallas Texas. He is also Founder and Presiding Bishop of *Word of Faith International Christian Center* in Southfield, Michigan. With the support of his lovely wife, Pastor Deborah L. Butler, and their children: Pastor André Butler and his wife, Minister Tiffany Butler, Pastor MiChelle Butler and Minister Kristina Butler, Bishop Butler continues to plant churches worldwide. He ministers extensively in churches, conferences and seminars throughout the United States and abroad with an emphasis on instruction, line-upon-line teaching and no-nonsense, practical application of God's Word.

Word of Faith International Christian Center
20000 W. Nine Mile Road • Southfield, MI 48075-5597
Tel.: 248.353.3476 • VP: 248.809.4306
24-Hour Prayer: 800.541.PRAY (7729)
To order: 888.909.WORD (9673)
wordoffaith.cc

More Books by
Keith A. Butler

Fresh Water Daily Devotional
ISBN: 978-0-9825028-6-0

The Art of Prayer
ISBN: 978-1-931939-27-0

Managing the Family Business
ISBN: 978-1-931939-28-7

God's Not Mad at You!
ISBN: 978-0-9825028-4-6

Living Life on Top: Winning Over Life's Challenges
ISBN: 978-0-9825028-5-3

Understanding the Kingdom of God
ISBN: 978-1-931939-29-4

Entering Into God's Rest for You
ISBN: 978-0-9825692-5-2

What To Do During a Financial Famine
ISBN: 978-1-931939-30-0

When the Righteous Are in Authority
ISBN: 978-0-9825692-0-7

TO ORDER CALL 888.909.WORD (9673)

CALLED TO MINISTRY?

This website is a place for ministry leaders to receive inspiration, revelation, encouragement, fellowship, ministry resources and more through our articles, video blogs, Leaders' Forum and eStore. Our heart's desire is to help you fulfill the vision of your ministry and truly TAKE FAITH to your world!

One of the goals of The Alliance is to establish a network of five-fold ministry gifts who are willing to not only receive from our ministry, but also who are willing to collaborate with other ministry gifts. Through sharing wisdom and successful ministry practices, we can help save the world together. For more information or to join The Alliance, please visit www.woficc.com/alliance.

CALL 248.353.3476 FOR MORE INFORMATION